MW01120600

Bringing Up John
©2012 by Ellen Walker

Published by RiverRun Select, an imprint of Piscataqua Press
142 Fleet Street | Portsmouth, New Hampshire 03801 | USA
603.431.2100 | www.riverrunbookstore.com

Printed in the United States of America

ISBN-13: 978-0-9885370-1-9
LCCN: 2012953920

www.piscataquapress.com

Bringing Up John

One Family's Life with Autism

*To Holly
Enjoy!*

Written by Ellen Walker

Ellen M Walker

Excerpts by A. H. Walker

Alan H Walker

With permission of John P. Walker

John Walker

Table of Contents

Do You Remember?

Do you remember when?

Can you go back that far again?

Are you willing to feel the joy?

Could you really hold back the pain?

How did you ever keep it together?

And stop from going insane.

Do you remember when

You got the news that day?

When that dark cloud came our way.

We didn't know what to do.

We didn't know what to say.

It just took us on a journey.

And this story will show you the way.

— A.H. Walker

Forward

After seven long years of waiting, my husband and I were thrilled to learn we were about to become parents. Sitting in the OB-Gyn's office that cold winter day, little did I realize what a fascinating journey we were about to embark upon.

Having recently become godparents to our baby nephew, we had some idea of what we could expect of parenthood. Our nephew was a contented infant who ate and slept on schedule and was generally very happy and pleasant. We watched him grow and dreamed of the wonderful experience we were in for.

Following an uneventful pregnancy and a rather quick delivery, our beautiful son John emerged from his peaceful, warm and dark cocoon inside of me into the bright lights and cool air of the delivery room. He immediately wailed his displeasure at such an abrupt transition into our world, thus beginning his lifelong struggle to accept the unexpected.

During John's early years his father worked long hours and was away from home much of the time. However, when his dad was able to be with us, John doted upon him. They began to form a very strong bond on the first night John came home from the hospital. You will find dad's dialogue in the following pages printed in italics so that it is easy to differentiate between two parents' varied interactions with our most precious and unique son.

At a time when Autism was almost unheard of, we began an experience that far surpassed any expectations we had of our role as parents. Within these pages lies our story, whose end we are unsure of, as it is still unfolding. If reading about our experiences can help even one parent to understand and accept their child on the Autism Spectrum, then our hard work will be immensely rewarded.

One

Our Beautiful Baby Boy

I have never felt better than the nine months of pregnancy I had with John. Each developmental step brought great pleasure and awe with what was happening inside of me. In 1979 there were few ultrasounds ordered and when they were done women seldom knew the sex of the child they were carrying. When I was four months pregnant, the doctor was concerned about the size of my uterus and ordered an ultrasound to determine if I had a multiple pregnancy.

As I drove to the hospital (there were no ultrasound machines in doctor's offices back then) my mind raced with anticipation about what the results would show. Lying on the cold, hard table my thoughts wandered. "What if the test confirmed the doctor's suspicion?" The ultrasound technician's voice snapped me back to reality. "I'm having a hard time tracking this baby. When I place the wand over the fetus, it moves away!" After much effort on her part, she finished up the procedure and sent me along to the OB-Gyn's office. Once there I was called into an examining room to learn the results. My heart pounded inside my chest . . . "Mrs. Walker", the doctor said, "There is only one baby." A sigh of relief escaped from my lips. He went on to explain that measurements taken during the ultrasound indicated that I was actually one month further along than originally expected. Our child would be born in early September instead of October.

The pregnancy progressed normally, at least we thought so. In hindsight I recall that whenever a hand was placed on my stomach the baby would move away quickly. Now I wonder if this was an early indication of autism. Right up until the ninth month of gestation my child was practically in constant motion. My belly often resembled the ocean's swells, rising and lowering repeatedly.

On the morning of my due date I had my final doctor's office visit. Everything was in place and I was sent home to await the first pains of labor. I had been extremely concerned for months that labor would be a nightmare! During the rest of the day I prepared for the impending addition to our family. I washed, dried and folded the laundry. Next I cleaned the house and as I was fixing lunch I began to experience some "cramping". Since this was my first pregnancy, I was unaware that what I really was feeling were early contractions.

These contractions continued throughout the day and by suppertime I began to realize there was a pattern to the contractions, signaling labor. By nine o'clock the contractions were coming every ten minutes or so. At this point I called my mother-in-law, who had eight children and therefore, in my eyes, was an expert in the field! She convinced me to call the doctor and he ordered me to go to the hospital. I remember that as I prepared to leave the house I went into the nursery where my packed suitcase was waiting. As I looked around the room I tried to imagine how much our life was about to change. There was no way to know what an incredible transition was about to take place.

My husband loaded my bag into the Jeep and I climbed into the front seat, ready to begin the journey. I often wonder how much the bumpy ride in a Jeep during labor impacted the length of time before John was born. We arrived at the hospital at 9:30 p.m. and were escorted into a labor room. The nurse came in and examined me, explaining that I was only dilated two centimeters. Knowing that ultimately I had to get to ten centimeters in order to deliver this child, this was a crushing blow! It seemed that we were in for a long night. The nurse asked me if I wanted any medication for the pain.

I declined the offer, preferring not to impact my newborn with chemicals. Labor was progressing rather slowly until the doctor arrived. After his examination he decided to "break my water". At 11 p.m. the baby's amniotic sac was ruptured by the obstetrician in order to speed up labor. The amniotic fluid was meconium stained which I now know can indicate fetal distress. Maybe it was a good thing I didn't understand this possibility at the time. The baby moved down very quickly and the next thing I knew the contractions were much stronger and coming on top of one another. My husband went to get the nurse who then checked my progress and exclaimed, "You're dilated ten centimeters, and I can see the baby's head!" She called for the doctor and off to the delivery room I was rushed.

A few pushes later, at 12:45 a.m., John entered our world screaming. The bright lights and cool temperature of the delivery room must have been an assault to his senses. John's Apgar score at one minute was seven and then at five minutes it improved to nine. After a quick bonding visit with mom and dad, our newborn was rushed off to the nursery, crying all the way there. I was taken to my room for a well-deserved rest. It all happened so quickly that it was hard to believe we were parents of a beautiful 8 lb. 13 oz. baby boy! We were on cloud nine - what a rush!

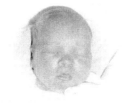

When John was brought to me the following morning I held my cherished bundle against my breast and he turned his head to look at me. (At least that what I wanted to believe.) There are no words that can describe the love and pride I felt at that moment. Even his piercing cries and difficulty feeding couldn't penetrate my euphoria. However, I was jarred back into reality when the doctor came in to tell me that our baby had become jaundiced. I thought his skin color was a little different but I didn't realize there was a problem. The doctor explained that his bilirubim count was borderline. He would discharge John only if we could make sure he was being exposed to sunlight that would help reduce his jaundice. Three-day old John was bundled up and discharged from the hospital for his ride home. Entering our home with our precious newborn baby we began the next chapter of our life as new parents. I often look back at the photograph that was taken as we stepped over the threshold of our home and into the world of parenthood. We stand in the doorway smiling broadly, our baby asleep in my arms. It seems a lifetime ago!

I'd always heard that if you have an easy delivery then you would have a difficult baby. Perhaps if I had believed that old wives tale, I would have been better prepared for the first few months of John's life. Settling in for our first day at home, John was placed in his bassinet which was positioned in front of two large windows. From this spot he was in the sunlight that his doctor said would be essential to cure the jaundice. He slept contentedly for a while . . . and then he woke up hungry. As I sat in a comfy rocking chair feeding my beautiful son his bottle of formula I had no idea what was in store for us. Before long this peaceful child was screaming and writhing in pain. It was almost impossible to get him to burp so gas built up inside of him with unbelievable force. Thus began my introduction to colic that I soon was watching rear its ugly head with each feeding. At first I blamed myself - after all I was a new mom and maybe I was doing something wrong. I suffered through that first day alone while John's dad slept peacefully before he had to work the night shift that evening. How he even slept through all that noise was testimony to his state of exhaustion that followed the whirlwind of activity surrounding our son's birth.

My aunt called to see how things were going and offered to

come by to help and possibly spend the night. How ridiculous, I thought! I could do this myself, sure that everything would turn out just fine. I soon realized what a mistake that was because shortly after my husband left for work all Hell broke loose! John woke up appearing to be hungry so I fixed him a bottle and sat down to feed him. Within minutes he began to twitch and stiffen up in my arms, shrieking continuously with his knees pulled up in pain. My emotions were quite raw in my postpartum state and soon I fell apart. A frantic call to dad at work brought him rushing home to rescue us.

Thank God that dad came through! He tenderly took John from my arms and sent me along to bed, emotionally and physically exhausted. Not once did I wake up that night, resting peacefully while father and son bonded in the other room. Upon awakening the next morning I learned that John slept very little his first night at home. The following is dad's impression of the events on that first night.

Hellooo, baby John! Now here I am, a brand new dad, holding this very alive little bundle of noise. Arms and legs are moving every which way. I knew I wouldn't have any trouble staying awake because I was used to being up all night, working the night shift routinely was part of my normal work schedule. However, I had zero idea of what was about to transpire this evening. My poor wife was completely exhausted, physically and emotionally and off she went to the bedroom. Now here I was sitting in my rocker recliner

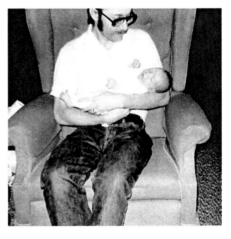

(you know, it was the old type that had large wings on both sides) so if I did fall asleep the baby could not fall out. It worked great

except we did not stay in that chair for very long periods of time. I held John in my left arm with his head on my left shoulder and he had his face against my neck so I felt every breath as we rocked gently. Now, I said to myself, this is great - it's a piece of cake . . . until I made the fatal attempt to stop rocking and just recline in the chair. NO DICE! Screams and hiccups with arms and legs amoving in all directions. Now I'm rocking again but it's not working. Instinctively I'm on my feet, walking up and down the hall, patting him on the back and jiggling him up and down. When all of a sudden, a giant belch came from this tiny little bundle and it leaked all over my shoulder. But the hiccups also stopped! Alright, this worked great but just then my nose picked up and odor I hadn't expected so soon in the evening. Oh yes, my first diaper change. This was the beginning of a pattern for the rest of my first night with baby John. ("Good morning Mom, thank God you're up!")

We learned from his first night's experience that movement seemed to soothe John when nothing else would. This was the first in a series of lessons John has taught us over the years.

Two

Mother Knows Best

For the next three months, the cycle of feeding followed by bouts of colic continued. Each time we went to the doctor I would tearfully explain what was happening. We were given a prescription for medication that seemed to ease the pain John had after he ate. However, it was not the answer to the problem. I asked the pediatrician over and over again if there was a chance my baby could be allergic to milk. The doctor assured me this would soon pass and urged me to continue with the milk formula. It was excruciating to follow the doctor's advice. I dreaded each feeding and the impending feeling of helplessness I felt as I watched John in distress. In desperation, when John was four months of age, I tried feeding him a soy-based formula. The difference was immediate, as well as incredible, and our baby was happy for the first time in his life. His smiles and coos replaced the horrible pain-filled screams. Life was good!

We continued to enjoy the newly present calm in the household as John grew and achieved developmental milestones either on time, or earlier, than the norm. I kept a journal to record his accomplishments and comments on what was happening as he progressed through infancy. I noted that by five months of age John rolled over from his stomach to his back. In fact, he managed to roll off the dressing table, but miraculously he was not injured. This incident made me realize the danger of allowing my eyes to stray from him for more than a second! During this time I also first wrote about John's love of music and its ability to pacify him.

When John was about six months old, he began to roll over and over in order to reach toys he wanted to play with. This became his way to get around until he began to walk. He never perfected his crawling technique, becoming frustrated with his attempts that only propelled him backward. He still was not sleeping through the night, getting up for a feeding around 3 a.m. I found it difficult to listen when other mothers boasted about their newborns sleeping all night when it seemed John would never do the same.

As John grew older we expanded his diet by adding apple juice. He loved the juice and drank contentedly. Unfortunately, his skin and scalp began to get blotchy and red. He always seemed itchy and would scratch himself until his skin was raw. We resorted to putting socks over his little hands in order to stop his incessant scratching. Again, the pediatrician said he felt there was no connection between the new diet and John's skin and scalp problems. The doctor gave us a prescription for cortisone cream to be applied to the problem areas and urged me to limit John's bathing. When I read the warnings enclosed with the medication, I was concerned about their long-term effect on John's health. Reluctantly, but religiously, I applied the cream desperately hoping for a miracle cure. John's discomfort made me feel helpless. When John was six months old I pleaded with the pediatrician for a second opinion. We were referred to an allergist, who agreed John could have food allergies. We switched to a hypoallergenic formula attempting to alleviate the problem. New medication was prescribed for John's allergies also. Dad recalls this experience:

Well, let me tell you that we never thought about how hard it would be to give medicine to a baby. This ordeal of giving John medicine became a two-person job. All of his medication had to be in liquid form. If it was only available in pills then they had to be crushed up and mixed with some kind of liquid so it could be swallowed. (Not so easy.) We had this plastic device that had a spoon at the top of a hollow handle with

What looks like cute, rosy red cheeks was actually horrible, itchy eczema caused by food allergies.

measurement lines for different amounts of liquid medication. The idea for this utensil was that you simply have the child open their mouth and you pour the medicine in and you're done. Well, the instructions didn't apply to the "Kung Fu Kid". The second the medicine touched John's lips his mouth shut and his arms and legs started thrusting, kicking and chopping at you. It took me to hold his head, and arms (don't ask me how I did this) while my wife held his legs and pinched his nose so he would open his mouth to put the medicine in. However, depending on what meds they were, he would spit them right out. After a while we figured out it was the taste of the medicine, usually the crushed-up pills, he refused to swallow. And then we remembered the old song about a spoonful of sugar makes the medicine go down . . . that did stop him from spitting the meds out but he still didn't like to take them. You still had to hold his arms to do this for about six months and then he was okay with it.

Immediately John's skin and scalp started to clear up. We were pleased to discover that under all that seborrhea John was sprouting beautiful red hair! (Later we were told that many children with red hair and fair skin have severe allergies!) John's skin glowed and he didn't scratch at himself any longer. His hands were free to explore his environment now.

The whole experience related to the food allergy episode made it clear to me that my intuition about John was valid. I firmly believe that a mother knows best what is going on with her child. The mother/child bond is stronger than any other I know of. It was an important lesson for me to learn and one I would remember for many years. I felt empowered by the realization that the countless hours I spent with John were essential in forming such a strong bond. I have never regretted my decision to put my career on hold in order to stay at home with my child.

Each new day my baby continued to amaze me. He never played with his toys for long, tossing them down frequently to find new interests. John was in constant motion, just as he had been inside of me. His attention span was extremely short so we were always looking for new ways to keep him happy. He loved to ride in the car, which came in handy on the days he was not quite himself. John had frequent ear infections from the time he was an infant throughout his childhood. He appeared to have a high tolerance for pain making it difficult to know that he was sick until the illness was well-established. Then he would fuss and pull on his ear which alerted me to his pain. Again, John taught me how to meet his needs.

Every day was a new adventure as he passed through the phases of early childhood development. He never did learn to crawl, preferring to move right onto "cruising", where he would hold onto furniture and step along. Not content to sit and play with toys, John would spend his time either rolling himself over to objects or cruising to reach things he found interesting. Some of those things were not in his best interest - but were more of an attraction to him than his toys. He even tried to make a meal of mom's snake plant one day when my head was turned!

At the age of nine months John was standing on his own and

he took his first step shortly thereafter. One beautiful Sunday morning we went to watch a boat parade after church. While we were at the park with Grammy and Aunt Teresa, John took his first steps in order to reach his auntie. We were thrilled at first but soon realized that walking only made it easier for him to find trouble! By the time John was a year old he no longer walked—he ran around like a little wild man, wreaking havoc all the way. Although his antics were funny at times, I fell into bed each night exhausted from hours of trying to stay one step ahead of John. I found that a momentary lapse of my attention could produce disastrous results!

For John's first birthday we had a party with many members of our large family present. I noted in my journal that John loved ripping open his gifts and was very interested in the colorful wrappings, sometimes ignoring the contents of the package. When the toys inside did catch his attention he would want to stop and explore each one. However, we were forced to keep him moving along to the next gift so his family would be able to see his reaction when he received their carefully chosen present. This was not at all okay with John (for good reason) and to add insult to injury he had to endure the first birthday cake rite of passage. Most babies would immediately dive into the yummy cake set before them - not so for John! He paid very little attention to the cake until his aunt picked up his chubby little hand and plopped it squarely into the gooey confection. . . Well, he screamed bloody murder and quickly extracted his limb from this tactile nightmare. John made us all aware of his displeasure and only calmed down when his hands were thoroughly washed and dried. After all the guests departed we were left with a very overwhelmed one-year old boy. We have a picture of John and his father sitting on the couch that night while Dad patiently tried to help him recover from this over stimulating day. Finally John was gently coaxed to sleep. In retrospect, this experience was one of the early indications of John's inability to handle too much stimulation which remains a struggle for him to this day.

John's development seemed to be pretty normal most of the

time and he was generally a happy child. His vocabulary consisted of many words including: cookie, cracker, Coke, bottle, etc. By the time he was twenty months old he was stringing words together and his first attempt at communicating his wishes was the phrase, "No go night!" That statement became his mantra and his activity level was incredibly frantic. Around this time John was diagnosed with allergic asthma. The medications that were prescribed increased his already frenzied pace. Life in our home became an exhausting round of administering medication, searching for allergen-free foods to feed him, and keeping track of John every waking minute to ensure his safety. How we survived all of this with our minds intact seems nothing short of a miracle.

Three:

Allergies & Asthma, Oh My!

We had only just begun to learn about what would become a lifetime of dealing with John's allergies. By the age of two he underwent skin testing to determine just what he was allergic to. The process itself was an ordeal . . . I held John down on the table on his belly while a nurse made a multitude of scratches on his back with a needle. Next, the serum was applied to each scratch and then the fun really began! John started reacting to the allergens immediately, becoming extremely itchy as the hives appeared. It was heart-wrenching to watch my child be tortured this way, but I also understood the necessity of the procedure. We were informed that his strongest reaction was to peanuts and tree nuts, with shellfish taking second place. In addition, John was allergic to cow's milk, eggs (both the yolks and whites), dust mites, pollen and mold. We had already figured out that apples were not his friend due to his experience with apple juice during infancy.

Trying to feed our toddler became an exercise in futility. Reading labels at the supermarket made us aware that most prepared foods contained milk and/or eggs, sometimes hidden behind words such as whey, lactic acid, albium, etc. Soon my husband and I became expert food ingredient detectives. My culinary skills were stretched as I struggled to find recipes that I could prepare to feed my

 highly allergic child. Family dinners and birthday parties were a nightmare! John wasn't able to tolerate milk (including cheese and ice cream), chocolate, nuts, and eggs, (one of the biggest hurdles to overcome because **everything** seemed to be baked with eggs) and so on and so on. We resorted to taking a survival bag of safe foods wherever we went. We desperately attempted to keep life as normal as possible despite these obstacles. John's exposure to animal dander left him with hives and difficulty breathing. Most of our relatives were pet owners so we were hardly able to visit anyone's home.

I remember the Fall that John turned two. Excitedly I put together a devil costume for him to wear on Halloween. It seemed appropriate, as he had become very active and daring. We called him "Baby Houdini" because he could escape restraints of any kind. It became necessary to use a harness that had clips on either side to snap onto shopping carts, the stroller, the high chair, the car seat and any other device he needed to be secure in. We even had to fashion a net to cover his crib because he would climb onto the rail and drop himself onto the floor. He sometimes fell, hitting his head on the floor in the process. Needless to say, the devil costume seemed to fit the bill for John's first disguise. We have a picture of him grinning with delight while modeling this costume. Unfortunately, he never got the chance to wear it on Halloween that year. Instead, John spent Halloween confined to an oxygen tent in the hospital.

Early in the morning on the day before Halloween, John became fussy, was feverish and began pulling on his ear. We took him to the pediatrician who diagnosed him with otitis media, or an ear infection. Antibiotics were ordered and we headed off to the pharmacy in pursuit of a magic formula to end the misery of our very unhappy child. John fought us tooth and nail but we eventually administered the medication, thinking we were on our way to a better place. However, as the day wore on he began struggling to breathe and was producing horrible squeaky sounds when he exhaled. This was our introduction to asthma (although in the beginning the diagnosis was bronchitis, and we later learned chronic bronchitis indicates asthma.)

Off we went back to the pediatrician's office, scared to death by John's struggle to breathe. He was immediately seen by the doctor, who explained that he had bronchitis and would need to have medication administered through a nebulizer.

This device is an air compressor with tubing attached through which medication is forced directly into the lungs. Unfortunately, in order to receive the medication one must use an oxygen mask to breathe it in. John wanted no part of that! We struggled to hold him still while this life-saving medication seeped into his lungs. The treatment seemed to help him for a while but not long after we got home he became sick again. When I called the doctor back he insisted we meet him in the emergency room of the hospital. So we set off for the hospital which, fortunately, was not too far away.

Upon our arrival at the emergency room John was evaluated and it was pretty clear he would need to be admitted to receive proper medical care. The next hour or so was a blur of activity which included obtaining a blood sample, urine sample, oxygen levels, etc. Although John was a very sick little boy, he still wasn't about the let anyone stick him with needles without a fight! So here I am, feeling helpless watching my child undergo numerous procedures as he screamed in fear and pain. It was devastating to witness John's disbelief of all that was happening to him. When he was finally taken to the pediatric ward we learned John would need to be placed in an oxygen tent to improve his breathing.

I will never forget the sight of my little boy standing inside that tent, arms outstretched and crying for me. With tears welled up in my eyes, I pleaded with the nurses to let me comfort him. They allowed me to hold John in my arms inside the tent, and zipped it closed around me. Only then did he calm down enough to fall asleep, exhausted from both the traumatic events this day had brought and his frightening struggle for breath. I can only hope that, due to his young age, any lingering memory of this horrible day has long been forgotten. I stayed by his side throughout his two-day hospitalization, never wanting him to feel abandoned in a strange and scary place. We were ecstatic when after a couple of days John was well enough to be discharged and left the hospital with two very relieved parents. It was a Halloween we will never forget!

After John's first hospitalization we became even more

cautious about any signs of respiratory distress so that we could hopefully avoid repeating such an ordeal. We monitored him closely, trying to keep life as normal as possible under the circumstances. A relatively routine Thanksgiving gave way to the anticipation of another enjoyable Christmas season with our beautiful two-year old son. John developed some nasal congestion, followed by a loose cough around this time. We continued his medication, hoping to avoid any problems with the asthma. Christmas Day he was thrilled with all of the excitement the holiday brings. His favorite gift was a wind-up record player that he played with for hours on end. Dad recalls the day he first introduced John to the real record player . . .

One day when John and I were home alone I put on a Beatles album. John loved music, as my wife mentioned earlier it settled him. But he never knew where the music came from (the record player) until the night I made the mistake of taking him over and lifting him up so he could see the record go around and around. My God, he got so excited that his arms were flapping like a bird and his legs were moving up and down so much I almost couldn't hold on to him for a second. He was in heaven. He was smiling and watching that record go around and around and when the music stopped it did not matter, as long as the record kept turning. I didn't think much about it until later in John's life, all I knew was he just plain loved it to death - to the point where I was stuck holding him there for hours until mom came home and that was enough for him to pull away from the record to play with her. I was thanking God mom came home when she did.

We thought all was well until the day before New Year's Eve, when John began coughing, wheezing and had difficulty breathing. Feeling a sense of deja-vu, we set off to the doctor's office for a visit that ended with another hospital admission. We went directly to the hospital from the doctor's office as we watched helplessly while our son struggled for each breath. The Emergency

Room doctor discovered John was suffering with another bout of otitis media (an ear infection) that had triggered his asthma. This admission was not as traumatic as the first, but an unpleasant experience, regardless. When John first saw the oxygen tent he declared, "No way!", but soon settled in and fell to sleep. John spent three days, including New Year's Eve, inside of an oxygen tent in the pediatric ward of the hospital. He was discharged on New Year's day and we left the hospital desperately hoping for the new year to bring better fortune to all of us!

Four

Lost Moments in Time

This chapter has been, by far, the most difficult I have written. It took me weeks to get up the courage to take myself back in time to the year between John's second and third birthday. Perhaps it was the trauma of the first hospital experiences or, more likely, my fear that I would not be able to account for all that happened during this time period. Just trying to keep John healthy was a full time job, not to mention the constant and very necessary vigilance overseeing his physical activity.

I noted in my journal on his second birthday "John is very, very active - almost constantly moving and running except for some quiet times when he will sit to look at his favorite books. John can be very sociable when he feels like it but will "tune you out" most of the time." When I wrote those words I didn't realize I was describing John's early characteristics of autism. I had absolutely no idea what those behaviors indicated. John's dad recounts his memory of John at this time with this excerpt he calls "Run, Baby, Run - Now I'm Cookin".

This little red haired boy was a cross between the Tasmanian Devil, beep, beep, the Roadrunner and bing, bing, bing, Ricochet Rabbit (not to mention Speedy Gonzalez, himself). He would run full speed forward, reverse and, oh yes, even sideways. If by chance he hit something on his way by it would just make him change direction and keep on moving - run, baby, run! I'd come home from work and my wife would be totally exhausted. I'd just say to her, "Was John cookin' all day?" and she didn't even have to answer! John's definition for running was "cookin". He got that from his Uncle Jeff at the beach one day and it just stuck with him.

John at two years old, happy and animated.

John at three years of age, note lack of expression on his face one year later.

As I've said right along, being caught up in the tide of never-ending medical interventions, along with exhausting hours spent chasing my energetic toddler left me in a state of mind where days just slipped by without much time to ponder the circumstances. Many times at the pediatrician's office I would question the doctor about the unusually active and somewhat abnormal behavior that I observed with my son, only to be told repeatedly "He's just a normal little boy". Well, it sure didn't seem normal to me, especially compared with many other children. No one else's child seemed to behave like John did. However, I pushed my intuition aside again and again, the doctor's words echoing in my ear, knowing deep down inside me that our life was anything but normal.

I continued to chronicle John's experiences in my journal, such as his first haircut (that poor barber's exasperation with trying to cut hair on a moving target). By all appearances my little boy was growing up. He had grown two and a half inches taller and gained four pounds in the six months since his second birthday. His physical size belied what were quickly becoming quite obvious developmental delays. Although John began talking early, he seemed to use less and less language to communicate. I began to notice that he no longer desired to communicate, verbally or otherwise.

John had two cousins living nearby that we spent a lot of time with. They both were less than a year older than him and it was very difficult not to compare the children's rate of development. At first many of his deficits could be chalked up to the fact that John was the youngest, but before long it became pretty clear to me he was lagging far behind. Toilet training was a nightmare! He had absolutely no interest in the potty chair, even when his favorite cousin began to wear "big boy underpants".

We would spend hours at the beach, park and playground during nice weather. We found it most helpful to keep John busy and active, although keeping him safe took a huge commitment. Most evenings I eagerly anticipated the peace and quiet that John's bedtime brought. He loved his bath time—and I would allow him a long period of time to play in the tub (he has always had an extreme fascination with water). Eventually he would wind down enough to fall asleep. I would peer into his room as he slept, his angelic face deep in slumber. It was a vast contrast to the mischievous ball of energy I had become so accustomed to. My heart would melt watching him sleep and the guilt would creep upon me as I recalled the day's events and my impatience that was displayed during the most stressful times. When given this chance to reflect I would wallow in self-pity, yearning to be the perfect mother - one who never lost her patience and faced each obstacle with smile on her face. The reality of the situation was that if I survived the temper tantrums, allergic episodes, food battles and everything else the day may have thrust upon me without losing my sanity, it was considered a successful day! I learned to leave the "Donna Reed" perfect mother model to those who had much less challenging offspring to raise. It became obvious that I was dealing with much more than the typical "terrible twos".

As John's third birthday approached it was hard to ignore the fact that he was not toilet trained, and he had no desire to be. I began to realize that John did not want to have a dirty diaper touching his skin and he would hide away to accomplish the dirty deed, quickly locating me afterward to change his diaper. Well, since he clearly knew when he had to go, I suspected he was capable of using the potty chair. His gig was up! Finally I got rid of all the diapers, explaining to him that he was a big boy and if he chose to mess his pants he would have to feel very uncomfortable. He pondered the thought of that tactile nightmare and immediately and completely became potty trained from that point on. His stubbornness was overcome by his realization of the physical discomfort he would have to endure. What a surprise!

John's third birthday passed by without much drama and we prepared for the upcoming holiday season. When the weather became too cold for outdoor exercise we enrolled in a gymnastics class to try to regulate John's activity level. He seemed to enjoy this diversion but it was clear he could not focus on the lesson being taught. As Thanksgiving approached, John's newest obsession was repeating the words "Happy Thanksgiving" over and over again. We could hardly wait for the holiday, and the phrase, to be over with. Interestingly, I noted in my journal at this time that John seemed to be behind in his verbal skills and mostly was repeating anything he heard.

John seemed excited about the whole Santa Claus/toy hype

surrounding the impending Christmas season. We continued our tradition of going to the tree farm to cut down our Christmas tree. John trudged along with us sharing in our pursuit of just the right specimen, one worthy of becoming our prized tree. We finally cut one down and upon arriving home we placed it in a prominent space in our living room. Our plan was to wait until the next day to decorate it. Well . . . we never did get that far because John almost immediately began to experience allergic symptoms and our attention was diverted to his medical needs. During the night John started to cough and wheeze, waking us up with his distress. I administered the appropriate medication and sat holding him in the rocking chair while waiting for his symptoms to improve. When they instead worsened, we called the doctor who advised us to meet him in the Emergency Room at the hospital. So off we went into the night, in search of the cure for John's ills. At the hospital John was given a shot of Epinephrine and a nebulizer treatment which miraculously improved his breathing. We were sent on our way by the doctor, who noted that the shot of adrenaline John had received probably meant the end of any hope for more sleep that night. Not long after we arrived home the cycle of breathing difficulty was repeated but this time, instead of being sent home, John was admitted to the hospital. Off to the pediatric ward and into the oxygen tent he reluctantly went. The allergist was called in, and he began to question us about any recent environmental changes at home. I nonchalantly mentioned we had been to the tree farm and brought home our Christmas tree the day before. BINGO! The doctor informed us that John was likely allergic to pine pollen, therefore creating his present problem. While I stayed with John at the hospital, his father went home to remove the offending tree from our house. He opened all the windows, allowing the frigid winter air to flush out the pollen particles that had permeated the environment.

John remained in the hospital for three days during the week before Christmas at which time he was so active the nurses had to resort to covering his crib with netting in order to contain him. After his discharge from the hospital we returned to a thoroughly clean house complete with an artificial Christmas tree waiting to be decorated by us. Fortunately, John was feeling much better by Christmas Eve and we enjoyed sharing the holiday season with family and friends. We looked forward to a New Year with much better luck than the prior one had presented.

Five

Help Me, Please!

As I have said in the prior chapter of this book, the year between John's second and third birthday seems such a blur. I was increasingly aware that John's development appeared to be delayed, or unusual in many ways. Although the doctor and his father, as well, were unconvinced I had a gut feeling that all was not well. John seemed to be very bright. He could count to 20, recite the alphabet and was able to sing many children's songs (such as Three Blind Mice and Twinkle, Twinkle, Little Star). He would memorize nursery rhymes and repeat them word for word, without hesitation, but his speech was difficult to understand. Children playing with John at the park would ask me, "Why does he talk like a baby?" His large stature belied the struggling psyche within. It was definitely time to address the problem, despite others' objections. I read in the newspaper about an upcoming screening for developmental delays in three year olds. The school department regularly conducted tests to determine if a child's development was progressing normally. I called to make an appointment and eagerly awaited the day when someone would either confirm or dismiss my fears about John. On that day I dressed John in his cutest outfit, wanting my child to make a good first impression. Well . . . he did impress everyone alright! Over and over again these professionals tried in earnest to assess his skills. And over and over again I was told he was unable to be tested because of his activity level. Only one tester made to effort to block out distractions in order to screen him, but even she said she couldn't determine the extent of his delays because of his inattention. Here I was with all of these strangers, who I expected would help me figure out what was happening to my son but no one seemed able to help me. Reeling from this devastating blow, I picked up my squirmy little boy and walked away from what I thought would be the answer to my prayers. On the way out I was told that if we could find a way to improve John's attention span he would be welcome to come back and try again.

Driving home my thoughts raced when suddenly I had an epiphany! John had become much worse behaviorally after each change in asthma medication. Maybe the allergist could help us figure this out. Thankfully, John's doctor had a pediatric background as well as the asthma and allergy expertise. When I called him he listened intently, suggesting we take John off all of the adrenaline-based drugs that were probably effecting his energy level. Although John certainly needed medication to control his allergic reactions, the doctor said we could try substituting a steroid medication regime for a two-week time frame. During those two weeks we discovered a remarkable difference in John's activity level.

Hurriedly, I contacted the professionals that were unable to test John earlier and asked for an appointment to attempt retesting. The assessment team later told me they would never forget the red-haired whirlwind who blew through the room during their first attempt. However, it was a different story the day the tests were finally administered. . . John was not the same child he had been two weeks earlier. During this evaluation he demonstrated global developmental delays, and his speech and language skills were determined to be his biggest challenge. The good news was that he could be enrolled in a five-week summer program where his needs would be determined and a plan to address them put in place. On top of that, while others tended to John's needs at school, I would have a little time to recharge my batteries.

Chapter 6:

A Welcome Respite

It was a gorgeous summer day as I dressed John in his Choo-Choo Charlie overalls and cap. We packed his essentials, including a home/school notebook (which would become my lifeline) into his little blue bag and stepped over the threshold of a new chapter in John's life. I stood outside of our house holding John's hand tightly as we waited for the little yellow bus to round the corner. John didn't hesitate to hop on board when the bus stopped in front of us. He seemed to be ripe for an adventure. I snapped a picture that morning which is permanently burned into my memory - my darling red-headed three year old boy standing in the bus doorway, waving goodbye with a smile spread across his face. Many have asked me, "How could you let your three year old go off on a bus all by himself?" I assured them that I was confident John would be safe, there was a bus monitor on board along with the driver and his teacher would be waiting to take him off the bus when he reached the school.

As the bus drove out of sight I breathed a sigh of relief. For the first time in almost four years I had time for myself. I was comforted knowing John would be in good hands while professionals evaluated his needs and determined the best way to address them. John really enjoyed the bus ride and did quite well his first time away from home. He seemed to flourish in the structured environment of the early childhood education program. At the end of the summer session we were told John had demonstrated significant delays in most areas of development, making him eligible to enter the year-round program in the fall. Wanting to foster friendships with the children he met in the summer program, we invited each of his classmates to his fourth birthday party in September.

Staff who had worked with John over the summer, as well as the professionals who would be working with him during the next year, met with me at the end of the summer program. As I walked into the conference room that day I was instantly overwhelmed by the number of people present. There were speech therapists, occupational therapists, and on and on. I found myself wishing I had my own therapist! It was emotionally devastating to hear each person report what was "wrong" with my child. Despite the initial shock I felt with each commentary, I left feeling encouraged that we had a plan to help John reach his potential.

Newly turned four, John was becoming even more

headstrong. I found it extremely difficult to manage his behavior. He was 42½ inches tall and 41 pounds of rough and tumble boy, out to get what he wanted! Only two weeks into the school year I was called for a meeting to discuss John's overly active and impulsive behavior. I had become so accustomed to dealing with John's behavior day-to-day that I hadn't even thought about how disruptive it would be in the classroom. I agreed a behavior plan could be instituted as part of his program but quickly dismissed any medical intervention to help control John's activity level. I was adamant that he was already taking too much medicine for his asthma and allergies and I was unwilling to add anymore medication to the mix.

There were daily notes written home that first year addressing John's lack of attention. His speech therapist tried valiantly to improve John's eye contact and to encourage his development of social skills. She reported that he would never initiate conservation and often was unresponsive when others tried to talk to him. However, I noted in my journal that by Christmas vacation he was talking a lot more and answering questions spontaneously. Surely those people working with John were miracle workers!

John was now 43 inches tall and weighed almost 45 pounds, placing him on the larger end of the spectrum for children his age. This fact made John's life problematic, as he appeared to be older than he was and therefore his delays were all the more obvious. We spent hours during the nice weather at various playgrounds and children there would be confused because John looked like them but acted quite differently. John seemed oblivious to their comments. Thankfully, John had cousins close to his age that he was able to play with often. Having known him since birth, they accepted John's limited abilities and didn't question his lack of skills. He was extremely comfortable with his cousin, Matthew, who actually seemed more like a brother than a cousin. They shared the common bond of being "only" children and enjoyed one another's company greatly.

Well, just when things were looking better for our young family, especially for John, we learned that the company where I worked for eleven and a half years was moving to Rhode Island. I was devastated! It was like losing a family member, not just a job. Our social life revolved around those people who worked with me. We were like one big family but what hurt the most was the loss of our incredible insurance coverage. The plan covered almost everything, from hospital stays to prescriptions and all of the specialists John was seeing. Although John had not yet been diagnosed with autism, he was continually being evaluated by many doctors who were desperately trying to figure out what was happening with our puzzling child. We could not move to Rhode Island because all of John's doctors and teachers were just starting to really communicate and understand John and the best way to work with him. I managed to find another job right away with a family-run business. One of the owner's sons took care of me and my family's insurance needs. For this I was, and still am, extremely grateful to him personally. Thank you, Jake.

John (and his teacher) made it through that first year of school with many gains noted. It was determined that, although he had made some progress, he was still very far behind most four year olds in his development. Thus, it was recommended he continue in the early education program for another year. He turned five in September and stayed at the preschool rather than going to Kindergarten. His teacher was well aware that John was bright and encouraged his love of written words. John had a word bank of fifty sight words he could read and more were added that year. A psychological exam was scheduled to determine what areas of his development needed to be addressed. The evaluation was done in October using a Stanford-Binet Intelligence Test. The school psychologist noted John's attention span and concentration were relatively short. He said that it became increasingly difficult to keep John task-oriented during this exam. At times John would "tune-out" the examiner. This occurred as the test items were becoming more difficult. John earned a mental age score of 5 years, four months which equates to an average IQ score of 96. The psychologist listed better attending skills and improved interactions with others, (rather than self-centered activities) as areas needing attention. He said John would probably have scored higher if he could have attended better. It was apparent to me now that John's learning was deeply affected by his inability to stay on task.

Our pediatrician and I discussed what to do about John's inability to focus. The doctor and I were both reluctant to start John on a drug called Ritalin, which was the drug of choice at the time to treat Attention Deficit Hyperactive Disorder. However, behavioral interventions being used at school were ineffective. John started Ritalin therapy and school staff were asked to note differences in his behavior. In March I received progress reports from John's teacher, speech therapist and occupational  therapist. All of them agreed the Ritalin seemed to produce better control of John's behavior. It surely wasn't a "magic bullet", but it made life with John more manageable. His teacher noted, "His overall behavior has improved in that disruptive, inappropriate outbursts have decreased to the point where we are able to ignore John, rather than having to remove him from the classroom." We chose to continue Ritalin therapy for as long as it seemed to help John function better.

As the second year at preschool was coming to an end, the task of finding the right placement for John's first grade experience began. There were many meetings where those who worked with

John debated which kind of learning environment would be best for John in first grade. I remember relaying my thoughts on John's disorder when a diagnosis had yet to be determined, explaining that it seemed as if a light switch would turn off his brain and he would check out. (When he was diagnosed with a seizure disorder later on I was surprised at my insight.)

After much soul-searching, the team decided John would benefit from a highly structured special education classroom with less than a dozen students. We braced ourselves for this huge transition. It was incredibly difficult to leave the people who we first we entrusted John to. Many tears were shed on John's last day at PEEP, both his teachers and I had a hard time parting. He wasn't nearly as concerned as we were, seeming to revel in the idea of attending elementary school. This scary adventure into the unknown was destined to begin, regardless of my hesitation. It was time to proceed into the next phase of John's education.

John at preschool with his first teacher, Helene.

Seven

A Bridge Too Far

Although we had spent hour upon hour huddled around the conference table at PEEP, debating what kind of supports John would require for his transition into elementary school, we were totally unprepared for what we found to be a gigantic leap of faith. I spent the summer before John entered elementary school trying to prepare him for his enormous evolution from the secure world of preschool into the vast obscurity this new chapter in his life was about to present. It was extremely difficult for me to leave behind the safety and trust I had become endeared to with those caring folks at PEEP. I tried desperately to disguise my fears and trepidation while John looked at this milestone as a positive experience. Unfortunately, rather than the secure bridge from preschool to elementary school we found instead a transition rife with unseen peril as we ventured across this unexpected chasm. I had been assured that adequate supervision would be provided to ensure John's safety. So I was appalled to discover he was on his own leaving the bus in the morning, following the crowd to the playground to await the opening of the school day. When I found this out I could hardly believe he hadn't been run over by a bus or something equally as horrible!

Upon approaching those in charge I was surprised to be looked upon as an overprotective parent rather than one concerned for the well-being of my son with special needs, both cognitive as well as medical. I tirelessly advocated for more support for John, which was continuously being denied by the same school staff who were reporting John's unusual behavior. It seemed as though John hardly knew what planet he was on most of the time, yet he was expected to function as independently as any other student. He repeatedly had his belongings stolen (snack and lunch included). The teacher would tell me she couldn't understand why John would stand underneath the water cascading off the corners of the school's roof. When asked for an explanation, John would offer that he was "taking a shower" (completely clothed)! Does this sound like a child able to take care of himself? I am all for fostering independence when it is done in a safe manner, but this was just plain ludicrous. I continued to plead with anyone who would listen, even using John's severe allergies as a case in point, to no avail. As a matter of fact, John's allergist was contacted and asked just how allergic John really was -- the doctor answered, on a scale of 1-10 John would be a 12!!!!

Even though the school was aware of John's allergies, he was exposed daily to tree pollen in the form of a very large Christmas tree erected in the middle of the school cafeteria. After coming home sick day after day, I investigated and was appalled at my discovery. Upon determining the cause of his sickness, I was told that I would need to come to school each day at lunchtime to eat lunch with John in his classroom. His teacher explained that if he couldn't eat with the other children in the cafeteria I would have to supply supervision of him while she had her lunch break. Why the offending tree was not removed in the best interest of a student's health remains a mystery to me. Equally as amazing was the lack of an alternative solution to this problem. As unbelievable as this situation seemed, I left work each noontime to ensure my son's well-being. This was probably about when I first realized I would have to become more aggressive advocating for my son. It didn't matter if people liked me or not, this was no popularity contest!

The last straw came when John chose not to board the bus after school one day, attempting instead to walk home. We lived at least five miles from the school, down a busy highway! I was waiting at home for his bus to arrive when the phone rang and I heard John's voice on the other end of the line. He wasn't making any sense in the words he repeated (naming the items he saw on the secretary's desk) as I screamed into the receiver, "John, John, where are you?" The school secretary got on the line and said, "John's trying to tell you he missed the bus." After asking incredulously, "How does a special education student miss the bus?", I told her I would be there shortly to pick John up. I later learned that, fortunately, a school employee who was working in a different program noticed John walking across the street from the school and inquired why he hadn't gotten on the bus. He then went to retrieve John, taking him into the safety of the building. Thank God someone was watching our for our son that day. There could have been a much more tragic end to this story. Upon arriving at the school, I gathered up my son and made sure everyone there was aware of what had just happened. I was sure to remind them that the school's liability was severely at risk. Amazingly, the very next day John finally had 1:1 support. Perhaps now we could rest assured that someone was watching out for his safety during school hours.

Eight

Battle Ends/War Begins

Sure, we may have won the battle that resulted in full time supervision of John during school hours but the war had only begun. During this crazy year of transition John had opted to pretty much check out of a world that made little sense to him. His behavior became even more odd and his preference appeared to be spending hours drifting off into some unknown place that was more comfortable to him.

I was totally unaware of the behavior control methods being used with John at school. He really didn't communicate much at this time and even if he did he probably wouldn't have disclosed the punishment he so greatly enjoyed. It seems that in someone's infinite wisdom a wooden box (open on only one side) was introduced into the classroom. When John would disobey he would be sent to sit in this container until he was ready to comply. Of course this afforded him the opportunity to "zone out" -- resulting in the punishment becoming a reward. I was horrified when I learned of this barbaric practice and immediately demanded a more appropriate form of behavior management. At this point a neuropsychologist was called in to observe John's behavior and help come up with a plan to deal with the problems. A neuro-psychologist is a doctoral-level psychologist who specializes in the study of brain-behavior relationships such as language, learning and memory, and higher level thinking called cognition. Thank God this doctor quickly realized that John's actions were unintentional and he encouraged further medical intervention. John's pediatrician promptly referred us to a pediatric neurologist nearby.

During our initial visit with this doctor, John's behavior was even more bizarre than his usual. My child was virtually ignored while the doctor grilled me about every intricacy of his development for what seemed like hours. After very little interaction with John and having observed him only in this setting, she declared to me that she knew what was "wrong" with our son. She then announced she had decided to diagnosis John with Autism and proclaimed that "what he was like today at seven years of age would be the same prognosis ten years from now at 17". I pleaded with her to investigate further, my mother's instinct was telling me that something else was amiss but she refused my request for an EEG (electroencephalography, a test that measures and records electrical activity in the brain) to be performed. Not only had this specialist given a diagnosis, when I asked for a source of written material that I could read to help me understand more about the disorder she quickly responded that I wasn't ready to research Autism. I was appalled that a doctor would think she should evaluate my readiness to research this information. I felt all hope for John was dashed and could hardly grasp the finality of the doctor's words. As I drove my son home that day I was totally devastated. Tears blurred my vision all the way home.

That Dark Day

Well, I remember that day as one of the darkest days in my early life. Now you must understand that men born in the fifties and sixties were raised to believe that men don't cry and men are

40

tough. They are protectors of women and should never show their feelings, and that professional people like doctors and lawyers and cops always know everything and always tell the truth. You should always believe them. Little did I know that my wife knew better, Thank God. That day my wife came home and told me what the doctor had said. All I could do was sit next to her and put my arms around her and let her cry. However, the next day when I was alone at home it finally hit me and my feelings just exploded. I wept like a snot-hanging, air-gulping child. I hadn't cried like that since I was about seven years old. Then I was so angry at God that I thought to myself, "was this blasphemy to do this?" I used to be an altar boy and was raised as a good Catholic boy, "Oh God, what do we do now?" This is where the real journey began.

Upon arriving home following the appointment, my inner voice urged me to call the pediatrician who had seen John since his birth. I explained the events of the day and he conferred with the neuro-psychologist who had observed John at school. They agreed with me that an EEG should be done and it was scheduled right away. I was about to find out what a sleep deprived EEG would entail.

Deja-Vu

Here I am again, just like that first night, staying up with John. I'm not trying to rock him to sleep this time, I'm trying to keep him awake for his sleep-deprived EEG test. I'll tell you that it was easier for me to stay up all night with John then it was for my wife because I was working a job that had a rotating shift schedule. But my wife and I rotated that night so we could both get some sleep. We were both exhausted but you could not stop my wife, she was on a mission. She was so determined to get to the bottom of this situation and to help John. She told me that doctor was dead wrong. And her gut feeling was right. From that day forward I never believed that all professionals were always right.

After keeping John awake most of the night and making sure he didn't fall asleep in the car on the way to the hospital, we finally arrived at the EEG lab ready for some answers to our many questions. John tolerated the procedure fairly well until the leads were removed from his scalp. His tactile overload came into play with the glue residue left adhered to his beautiful red hair. John can still recall his aversion to this unwelcome consequence of the test and I can remember the hours he carefully excised each offending speck of glue. We made our journey back home, caught up on our sleep and eagerly awaited the results of the test.

A few days later I received a telephone call from the pediatric neurologist explaining that brain wave abnormalities were detected during the EEG. Remember, this was the doctor who absolutely dismissed my suggestion that further testing might be useful. She desperately tried to disguise her error in judgment by using terminology she thought would be beyond my range of knowledge. I was told there was "spike activity", "elytriform discharges" and any other wording besides seizures. She recommended that John begin taking a drug called Tegretol to "help with his behavior". I recognized the name of the medication as an anti-seizure medication at which time her gig was up. I could not trust a doctor who wasn't able to admit her error --- John's pediatrician agreed and referred us to a pediatric neurologist at Boston Children's Hospital.

By now it was July of 1986 and that first fateful elementary school year had ended. We soon found out that John had been experiencing seizures with alarming frequency which explained the "unusual spells" in school. The neuropsychologist's suspicion was confirmed. After a second neurological examination and review of the EEG, John was diagnosed with Landau-Kleffner Syndrome or "acquired ictal aphasia". Landau-Kleffner Syndrome is a childhood seizure disorder that falls within the Autism Spectrum. When left undiagnosed, or untreated, it affects the child's ability to speak and understand language. I was told by the doctor at Children's Hospital that the drug of choice to help control these seizures is Tegretol. The dose of Tegretol prescribed by the first doctor was determined to be sub-therapeutic and his dose was increased accordingly. The Boston doctor questioned "additional attentional difficulties" that he felt were "amendable to Ritalin therapy". He provided us with copies of several articles explaining this disorder. I went on to conduct further research in an effort to better understand why John did the things he did and to learn how I could help him cope. At last we had hope that medication to control John's seizures could result in increased awareness and improved communication skills.

Over the summer I noticed many changes in John. He was much more alert and interested in what was going on around him. He began to talk a lot more and seemed so much happier. Our family went on a vacation to the mountains where we thoroughly enjoyed our newly transformed son. Don't get me wrong, it wasn't all peaches and cream. John still struggled with impulsiveness due to his ADHD. He did then, and still does, struggle with over-stimulation of his nervous system, which is a hallmark of Autism. Although communication was much improved, he still needed a lot of support in this area.

Upon further research into this relatively rare disorder called Landau-Kleffner Syndrome, I learned that John's early intervention at the preschool special education program probably saved him from going through life unable to communicate verbally. A report I read said that often, once a person with this disorder loses all of their speech, they may never regain it. Although we weren't aware of this diagnosis when he was at PEEP, he had begun speech therapy before he lost all of his language skills. The echolalia seemed to be the last stronghold of his language function, and thankfully he could still repeat words he heard.

I spent most of that summer learning more and more about this complex disorder. The events of John's life after two years of age began to fall into place. As I read the information I was amazed to feel that these articles could have been written about John. It was comforting to read that many of these children went on to live somewhat normal lives. I became immersed in this newfound world, communicating with other parents who have children with this diagnosis. John was even part of a study trying to identify the cause of Landau-Kleffner Syndrome. I spent hours compiling information about John's development and his early experiences. The questionnaire seemed to be infinite pages long! I received a letter months after I had returned the questionnaire. It seems that the only common thread found between all of the participants in this study was the fact that all of them lived near large bodies of water. Does this indicate an environmental factor? Could mercury play a part in the fate of these children? We probably will never know the whys and hows of Landau-Kleffner Syndrome.

At some point I was able to move on from searching for the cause of my son's disorder, to realizing that John is who he is and that's perfectly fine. He has many positive attributes despite his struggles living in a world he finds overwhelming and confusing at times. He has incredible artistic talent and could draw almost anything at a young age. His memory is amazing! We hope someday John will find his niche in society. This syndrome falls within the spectrum of Autism and many of his character traits mirror those of people diagnosed with Asperger's disorder. Now that we knew what we were dealing with it was time to find appropriate educational approaches to help John succeed in school.

Nine

Obsessions

Before I go on any further, I am feeling the need to address a characteristic children on the Autism Spectrum often exhibit. It seems they are forever becoming obsessed with one thing or another. One of John's first obsessions was anything to do with the Peanuts character, Charlie Brown. The author, Charles Schultz, surely never knew what an influence he had on our son! When John showed such a strong interest in this, I thought it would be a cute theme to decorate his bedroom with. John just took it from there - he ate, slept and lived Charlie Brown. He would spend hours with movies, books, TV shows and whatever else was available to feed his obsession. His preoccupation with this affected all aspects of his life.

Espanol, Charlie Brown

John was so into Charlie Brown, as my wife has stated. Well, let me tell you that I had something most people didn't have at this time. It was a video disc player that happened to have the ability to play a movie in both Spanish and English. Oh, my God! I thought I was going to go totally insane hearing all of my favorite Snoopy characters talking and singing in Spanish over and over again. John would beg me to play these movies every time we were home together by ourselves. The only way to talk him out of this was to play records or tapes in the new cassette recorder/player. He loved to watch the needles bounce up and down on the volume gauges of the cassette player. He loved this as much as he loved watching a record going around and around.

Although John seemed proud of his painting, his face shows no emotion.

I believe Charlie Brown was the vehicle for John's later fascination to learn to speak Spanish. Since we just touched on the record fascination, I should probably fill you in on what it has meant to John. John absolutely loves music, and he knows everything about it. He has an extreme ability to memorize trivia about things he is interested in. Well, he can tell you anything you ever wanted to know (and lots of times, things you could care less about) concerning recording artists. He knows all the record companies, who recorded the music, when the recording was done, etc. etc. etc. John could be a musicologist with his vast knowledge of this field. He began his lifelong hobby of collecting records as a young boy. He would request records be given to him for any gift-giving occasion and soon family members started to pass along their record collections to John when new media, such as cassette tapes, and then CDs, became popular and they no longer had much use for their records. John would be delighted with every donation. Over time it became more difficult to acquire new material so we started to peruse yard sales and flea markets in search of records to add to John's collection. As a matter of fact, John collected so many records that his room was quickly becoming crowded with them. John's dad made several wooden boxes to hold his collection, which now spilled over into our hallway.

During this time we were still living in a mobile home that was pretty small. John's room resembled a closet in size, and his father even removed the built-in closet to give him more space. However, John had never lived anywhere else and so he didn't seem to mind the cramped quarters. While shopping at flea markets John became enthralled with old soft drink bottles. He always has been interested in different products and their logos so this new interest soon became the next hoarding activity John engaged in. He collected many bottles and again Dad came to the rescue by making wooden cases to hang on John's bedroom walls to display this new collection. This hobby continued for several years and as quickly as he began his fascination with old bottles, he lost all interest in them. When we moved to a larger house (about the time he graduated from high school) we packed the collection away and he chose not to unpack them, but store the boxes in our shed. In contrast, record collecting continues to be one of his most favorite activities to this day. We spend every Saturday during good weather checking out all the area yard sales. I swear John can sniff out record albums because he is immediately drawn to them, even if the records are located in a box under a table! John's eagle eye is always trained on the various assortment of items at each yard sale and he often tells me there are records for sale even before we approach the sale. An added benefit of this activity is the practice of money skills necessary in order to purchase new records. For a long time I tried valiantly to teach John about money and it's values without much success, but this real life experience has certainly been a vehicle for him to learn this valuable life skill.

Ten

Time to Move On!

Although John had been diagnosed in Boston, my husband and I yearned for a doctor closer to home who would tend to John's neurological needs. After the horrible experience we had with the pediatric neurologist in our area, we were relieved to find a neurologist who normally didn't see pediatric patients but agreed to see John and coordinate our son's care with the doctor at Boston Children's Hospital At our initial visit with this new doctor, John actually had a seizure during his examination. The neurologist promptly increased John's Tegretol dose to a more appropriate level that would decrease the number of seizures John was experiencing. With the medical end taken care of, we began to focus on his education.

John's educational team had agreed in June he should stay in the same program he had been in the previous year, moving up to the next level. This was a small, self-contained classroom that afforded close supervision and attention to his needs.   With periodic adjustments of medication and behavioral supports, John seemed to do fairly well in school. He could read very well but struggled with math concepts. John was already familiar with his classmates because the group of children moved along together from one year to the next. John's social skills were also a big problem for him but, because this class had fewer students than mainstream classes, his teacher and aide were able to facilitate peer relationships. More time was spent on tailoring instruction to meet each child's individual needs.

During November of that year John was presented with another challenge when his grandfather passed away. It was difficult for John to understand the finality of death. We tried to explain it in every way possible and visited the gravesite quite often, hoping to allow John's grief process to begin. However, each time we went to the cemetery, John would insist that we should bring along blankets (Grandpa was cold) and food (Grandpa was hungry). We had little success convincing John that, according to our religious beliefs, his grandfather's spirit had left his earthly body and was now in Heaven. Clearly, he had a difficult time with this abstract notion. Suddenly, I thought of an idea that seemed like it might work. We went to a store, purchased a balloon and returned to the cemetery with it. I urged John to release the balloon so it could go up to grandpa in Heaven. As we watched it's ascent into the sky, John finally seemed to comprehend what we had been saying all along. He was happy to send grandpa a balloon. It was amazing that his simple solution allowed John to let go of the anxiety he had harbored since this tragic event, replacing it with a feeling of peace.

Glad and Sad

It was late in 1985 that I received a call from a local power generating plant saying they had wanted to hire me a year ago but they had misplaced my resume. Now they wanted to know if I was still interested in a job there. I was ecstatic and accepted the job after a brief interview. This was a dream come true for our family. The benefits were great for us, especially the health insurance. The downside was that this new job had a rotating shift schedule so I was not at home with my wife and son a lot of the time, like I had been the past two years. In 1986 my father passed away and I was devastated. What really upset me and my wife was how much his death upset our son, John. He just could not grasp it. Well, my wife explained how she dealt with this dilemma. Amazing what a 25 cent balloon and an intuitive idea can do!

As the school year moved along, the task of determining the most appropriate placement for the next academic year began. John's teacher reported her concerns about having John continue in the program he was in. Most of the other children in his class were functioning far below John academically, especially in their reading skills. She went on to explain that she had set up an individual reading program for John because no one else in the class could read at his level. I will always be grateful that this educator identified his need and acted upon it. She could have easily allowed John to spend the year bored stiff. She went on to share that there was little chance of the situation changing in the year to come. The children in this class would move along together through each level of this program. So a new, more appropriate, placement was sought for John.

As part of this process, a new psychologist was brought in to test John. This doctor had never even seen John, and spent only an hour with him to complete the examination. His summary was full of concern that John had an obsession with death (keep in mind that his grandfather had recently died) and there were many questions about his thought process, due to the "stories" he told. I found it interesting that this doctor didn't seem to be aware of the penchant children with Autism have to repeat word-for-word any script they have seen or heard. Most of the "stories" listed were related to cartoons and movies John had seen. As I read through his report I was amused with John's very literal answers that were misinterpreted as those of someone with a thought disorder. Obviously people with Autism do not do well with the Rorschach ink blot test. For instance, when John was shown an ink blot that resembled a butterfly the doctor thought it odd that he "ruined" the usual response by calling it a rotten butterfly. I'm fairly certain that John thought of butterflies as colorful creatures, therefore a black one was no longer alive and probably had started to decompose. Anyway, I dismissed any findings brought forward from this test because I felt that the examiner had very little knowledge of the way children with Autism function. I never understood why this psychiatrist was asked to test John when the neuropsychologist who had tested John a year earlier was currently in the process of administering another neuropsychological assessment. He saw John on three separate occasions, halting the testing when John became distracted or uncooperative. I thought his report was a more accurate example of John's developmental level.

When John's educational team met to discuss the next year's placement, it became clear to me why the new psychologist was called in. It seemed that because John's current placement was deemed inappropriate and there were few options available, the program being suggested was one for students who are emotionally handicapped. When I was approached by the team to discuss the possibility of John attending that program, I was told his code would need to be changed from "speech and language/other health" to "emotionally handicapped" in order for him to go there. There was no way I would agree to a code for my child that was not accurate. The fact that John had behavioral issues seemed to validate their decision for that placement. Amazingly, John was the first student placed in this program who was not coded as emotionally handicapped. I was assured John's behavior plan would differ from most of their students. I reluctantly agreed to allow this move after visiting the classroom. I felt a little better about it after meeting the teacher and watching how the program was run. His new teacher seemed very nice, as well as flexible, (an important attribute considering John would not have the same needs as her typical students). I realize now what a big mistake I made that year and, in retrospect, I feel I didn't advocate strongly enough for a more appropriate educational experience for John.

Although the staff tried to meet John's needs, I feel this placement was inappropriate. I spent the next two years feeling guilty for agreeing to have him placed there.

After John's first day in the new program, he returned home and immediately lay down on the floor, kicking his feet and pounding his fists. When I asked him what he was doing he said, "Sit on me, that's what the teachers at school do to the kids." He had little understanding about the out-of-control behavior he saw and was confused by the restraint techniques that were used, out of necessity, to keep everyone safe. Although this initial experience was alarming, John did settle in and, at the very least, he was being academically challenged. There were more instances when he shared disturbing word-for-word accounts of what was happening at school.

Unfortunately, John learned more about life than I would have liked him to while in this classroom. He was a master of imitation and he began to have new behavioral issues. When I was reading his home/school notebooks in order to recall the experiences we had at this time, I noticed that there were many references to John's inability to focus during class. I'd forgotten that, in addition to a poor placement, he also was dealing with medication issues. The doctors and I were trying hard to find the right dose of ADHD medicine to help John with his impulsive behavior and allow him to pay attention better. This is never an easy task and, with John's sensitive chemical balance, it was a real struggle for him. I can only imagine what it's like to have so little control over the choices you make. Unfortunately, the behavior was inappropriate and he had to deal with the consequences of his actions. John would need to learn strategies to help him make it through each day. We found that using visual schedules and checklists could make all the difference for him. Establishing a routine, and sticking to it, seemed to calm John down and make this time more bearable.

John's teacher his first year in this program was pregnant and left on maternity leave midway through the year. This necessitated an adjustment to a substitute teacher. A man was hired to take the teacher's place, this being the first time John had a male role model in school. It proved to be such a positive experience for John that we realized a male influence would be beneficial for him throughout his schooling. At any rate, John made it through the "teacher switch" relatively unscathed. His original teacher returned from her maternity leave and finished out the year with John. Although I voiced my concerns at meetings about the following year's placement, I was told that John would have to stay in the program another year because there was no better place for him in the school system. If he hadn't had such wonderful teachers in this program I would have found the situation unbearable long before I did. His teacher the following year was also very flexible and tried very hard to meet his needs. John continued to do well academically and was able to work on his social difficulties within the program. Social groups met each morning and John practiced new skills. However, as the year progressed it became much more clear to me that John was confused by the difference between other students in his class and himself. He was also becoming somewhat ostracized by the rest of the school's population because of his association with this program. One night I brought John back to school to attend a concert. After it was over I was talking with John's teacher when he asked if he could go out to the playground while he was waiting for me. Reluctantly I agreed, knowing I would join him shortly. When I went to pick him up I was appalled at what I saw. Another student outside with him was calling him a retard.

He used that horrible name instead of John's own when addressing him. The saddest part of it was that John didn't realize what was going on. He just was happy a peer was talking to him. Well, I nearly came unglued hearing the remark! I marched over to the fence and asked the kid who he was talking to. He replied that he was talking to "that retard over there". I immediately informed him that John was not retarded and added that John was probably smarter than him. I was so furious as I took John to the car. He was confused about why I was so angry and I hesitated to explain because I didn't want him to feel badly, knowing he had clearly missed the insult. This was one of the times I found it hardest to be John's mom. I hurt for him even though he was oblivious to the insult.

I continually requested a better placement for John. Near the end of the year I became embroiled in a huge fight to have John moved to a local private school which dealt with children who had language disorders. The tuition was expensive but I felt strongly that if the school department didn't have an appropriate program for John, he would have to be educated out of the district. After all, according to federal law he was entitled to a free and **appropriate** education. The school psychologist advocated for John and together we convinced the other members of John's team that this would be a much better placement for John next year. Finally we succeeded in getting John enrolled in the private school for their summer program where their staff could determine whether their school was a good place for John to attend full-time in the fall.

The summer between John's public and private school experience was an eventful one. John's grandmother was spending time at a campground that we visited quite often. He loved to go there, especially when we invited a buddy to come along. Dad came to visit on a day off and he never quite recovered from an experience he had with John there. He and John were in the locker room, preparing to use the pool. Upon observing an elderly gentleman who was changing his clothes, John said (with his usual blunt honesty), "Mister, you have a wrinkly old penis." The man replied, "Well, I've had it for a long time." Dad said he thought he would die when John said that and he never left the campsite again for fear he would see that man. I've learned to accept that John often makes inappropriate comments about what he observes. Over the years, it has been my feeling that if people can't figure out what's going on, it's their problem. John is who he is and we can't change him, nor would we want to. Later we explain to John (in private) how what he said may have made the person feel badly and then we encourage him to try to think before he speaks. We realize his impulsivity will probably dictate the outcome of most interactions. Unfortunately, John seems to have little control over these situations.

John, age 10, taken outside of his new school. Learning Skills Academy

Another experience we encountered that same summer was one we call "John's adventure". One day while visiting Nana at her house, which is about twelve miles from our own, John suddenly disappeared. While my mom and I were saying our goodbyes he just vanished. We called his name and searched all around the house for him. But he was gone. Our anxiety escalated and we called the police. They arrived shortly thereafter and began a search. I was asked to remain at the house in case they found John while the police and their dogs went out into the woods behind the house to look for our son. A frantic phone call summoned Dad and his brother, who went driving along the back roads looking for any trace of John. Nearly three hours later a truck pulled into the driveway and the driver pointed to John sitting beside him and asked, "Are you looking for this guy?" Relief flushed over me. John's father, who rarely showed very much emotion, collapsed onto the hood of his truck and sobbed. John seemed perplexed that we were so upset. He said he was only trying to find the music store he so dearly loved to visit in a nearby city. John said he realized he was lost when he emerged from the logging road in the woods behind Nana's house. He then followed the power lines, finding a path that led to a housing development. John saw a man who was mowing his lawn and told him he was lost. When questioned about where he lived, John promptly repeated his address, which he had memorized in case of an emergency. The only problem was that he was far from home, visiting his grandmother in her small town. The man (who incidentally, was wearing a Special Olympics volunteer shirt) took John in his truck and attempted to have John show him the way back to his grandmother's house. He asked John what his grandmother's name was and the reply was, "Nana." We never gave a thought to telling John what his grandmother's full name was. When he didn't seem to be getting anywhere close to helping John find his way back home, he decided to take John to the police station. On their way there, they passed my mother's house and saw all of the police cars on the lawn. Voila! This must be the house, he decided. We are forever grateful for that good Samaritan. I hope no one else ever has to have this experience! It only takes a minute for a child like John to make a very poor judgment and put themselves in severe danger. I used this story to explain my concern for John's safety and to advocate for extreme supervision in his new school.

Total Panic

You cannot believe what a call like the one I got from my wife telling me that John was missing does to you and I hope it never happens to anyone. From the moment you hear those words (your child is missing) you are in absolute shock and total panic. After I hung up the phone I just sat there for a minute and then immediately called my brother, Thomas, to help in the search for John. We both knew all the back roads in the area around my mother-in-law's house. I drove around in disbelief of what had happened and looked in the woods on both sides of the road as best I could. I was talking to myself continuously, fighting back my tears all the way because they might blur my vision and I might miss seeing John. The darker it got the worse my state of mind was. Now it was totally dark and I was ready to break so I headed back to my mother-in-law's house. That's when I saw all the police cars and people in the driveway. As I drove up I finally saw John with my wife and I just got out of my vehicle and ran over to them and you know the rest!

Foster's Daily Democrat, Dover NH
Friday Evening, August 25, 1989

Lost boy in Eliot finds way back to grandmother

ELIOT, Maine — The 10-year-old boy who wandered from his grandmother's home Thursday night returned unharmed an hour after he was reported missing.

John P. Walker of Portsmouth, N.H., walked into the woods near the State Road home of his grandmother, Marice Barzal, around 6 p.m. and began a longer journey than he had expected.

"We've had him out in the woods before and he's been all right, but you never know," explained Mrs. Barzal. The family was concerned because John suffers from severe allergies to plants and trees.

Mrs. Barzal said that John went for a walk and came upon a logging road which he took, following the tire tracks from dirt bikes. He ended up in someone's backyard and told a man there where he lived and that he was lost.

While John sat in the man's pick-up truck searching for home, Eliot police, three Portsmouth police officers and two dogs responded to the missing persons call made at 6:30 p.m. by John's mother Ellen Walker. Standing by were Eliot and Kittery fire departments.

"My house is not far from the police station," Mrs. Barzal said, "so when they rode by, they saw all the police cruisers in my yard and found home."

Though relatives were nerve-wracked by the experience, John found his walk to be an interesting experience.

"He said it was a great adventure," John's grandmother said. "For him it was a great thing to do, but for us it was something else."

Acting Police Chief Charles DeCristo said because the boy was in unfamiliar territory and was last seen heading into the woods, the darkening sky precipitated the search.

Even though the private school had very small classes, it was determined John still needed 1:1 assistance. This discovery was not very palatable to the school district, who now would have to pay tuition to the private school, and the salary for a person to help John. At last all of the arrangements had been made for John to become a full time student there in the Fall. It was a wonderful late summer day when John began his first day at the new school. He was lucky to have a teacher who taught phonology part time to be his 1:1 assistant. She worked very well with John and was able to effectively include him when he was ready but also knew when John needed a quieter or more slow-paced learning experience. Most of the children attending this school had some degree of a learning disability. John was one of the younger students and the older ones sort of looked out for him and encouraged his efforts. This school had some very innovative teachers who created lots of different methods of learning. They organized activities to make lessons more hands-on and fun. Then they would plan learning fairs for the students to demonstrate what they had discovered. John blossomed in this environment. There were some problems, mostly brought on by John's impulsivity. One boy, who the other children were afraid of because he would lash out unpredictably when he was angry, was the target of one of John's spontaneous actions. John had chosen a juice box that was called green slime, which was popular at that time because of the movie Ghost Busters. In retrospect, I should have known better than to send it to school with him. One day during lunch, John marched up to the bully and squirted the contents of the juice box over that boy's head. The other children stood by in awe of John's fearlessness while the object of John's mischievous stunt reeled in shock at this assault. He had never been challenged and didn't know what to do. It didn't take long for a staff member to intervene before disaster struck. Needless to say, John was immediately punished for his insensitivity. He still laughs to this day when remembering this experience even though he got into trouble I guess it was worth it to him.

I was close friends with several of the other moms whose

children attended this school. Most of them traveled quite a distance with their child each day and so they sort of hung out in the area until the end of the school day instead of making the trip twice. I lived right down the street from the school and my house became a place for our informal support group to meet. We shared our talents and each of us taught the others how to do a particular craft. One mom showed us how to make pierced lampshades, and the others followed suit. It was an enjoyable time for us to unwind while our children were being well taken care of, their individual needs being met at the school. I am grateful for the support those women provided me and for the very dedicated teachers who tried so hard to help John reach his potential. For three years things went along pretty smoothly. John seemed to flourish in this environment and made some significant gains overall. Students were bussed to the school from many districts in New Hampshire.

The school had a very good reputation and provided many opportunities John would not have otherwise experienced. They didn't have a gymnasium so their physical education program consisted of alternating a day each week at a private gymnastics club with field trips planned on the opposite weeks. John was fortunate to experience downhill skiing, canoeing, participating in a ropes course, and many other activities. He always enjoyed sharing his escapades with us when he returned from these adventurous field trips. On one canoeing trip we learned that the canoe overturned and everyone and everything got thoroughly drenched. Unfortunately, John's medication was in his backpack and it dissolved into the napkin I had placed it into. In desperation, staff panicked about how he could receive his much needed seizure medicine and opted to have him chew on the napkin with the hope John would absorb the medication. That experience stands out in my memory because it was so comical to try and picture that scenario. Another time John came home with a videotape of him doing the ropes course. Even though he was sitting beside me as I watched it, I held my breath as I saw him jump from tree to tree and walk across a log that was many feet above the ground. John got accolades from his peers on that trip because he showed absolutely no fear and many of them were unable to overcome their apprehension to be able to participate.

As John matured he began to have some difficulty with behavior control again. It seemed that when the hormones kicked in, his delicate chemical balance became unhinged. At one point he was hospitalized for evaluation purposes, resulting in another misdiagnosis. John and I spent five summer days in a prominent Boston hospital while he was undergoing a long term EEG. It wasn't easy for him being tethered to a bed by the electrical leads attached to his head. I opted to stay with him, sleeping on a cot at the foot of his bed. A neuropsychopharmacologist was called in to determine what medications were working and whether some should be changed. He observed some symptoms he felt were in the realm of schizophrenia and told me that John was hearing voices. When questioning John about this, it was hard to tell if he understood what we asked because of his literal nature. Of course everyone hears voices all the time!

However, this doctor wanted to change John's diagnosis from Landau-Kleffner to schizophrenia. He wanted to admit John for a ten day inpatient stay in the psychiatric unit, which we refused to allow. I could hardly believe what was happening. When we arrived home, I called several of the doctors who had been seeing John right along and they were as astonished as I was with this new diagnosis. We were referred to another psychiatrist where it took a year (during which John had many medication trials) to undo the travesty brought on by the doctor in Boston. Finally, John was put back on his anti seizure medication and, thankfully, the ADHD medication was restarted. Life was good once again!

Eleven

Cub Scouts

One of John's greatest childhood social experiences came in the form of belonging to the local Cub Scout pack. A good friend of mine, Judy, was a den leader for her sons' Cub Scout pack and she urged me to allow John to attend a meeting at her house. I was skeptical but he was excited to try it out and he had a blast at that first meeting! Judy said the meeting went well, however, he'd likely need more assistance. Evidently she spent a good deal of time working closely with John, which didn't leave much time with the other boys. By now I was working in special education and one of my friends from school volunteered to accompany John to his scout activities. Linda met us at there, at which point I would leave. John greatly enjoyed the activities and this was an opportunity for him to feel part of a group. For the next couple of years he reveled in a sense of belonging and also quickly mastered the various skills scouting teaches. At Pinewood Derby time John's dad gladly jumped right in.

Cub Scouts

I was so proud when John was in the Cub Scouts. Number one, because I was a scout myself. But the real reason was, being the parent of an autistic son, it's really hard when you are at work and you have to listen to all of your coworkers talk about their son's achievements in school and in sports. They keep bragging all the time and you just have to listen or walk away. I know they were not trying to be hurtful but it just hit home. So now I would be part of the group, it was great! Pinewood Derby, Oh ya!

Oh ya, this was something I could really get into. I remember when my dad helped me with the building of my race car. You know when I think back to then all my dad had for us to build my car was a jack knife to hand carve the body and a hammer to put the wheels onto the car. He let me paint it green. I was happy, but it didn't go very fast and it didn't last long in the competition.

Well, I learned a lot later on about how to build those derby cars. I had a workshop with all the power saws , belt sanders, and all the equipment including the most valuable thing of all, which was an accurate scale to measure the weight of the car to the ounce.

I hope you realize that most little scouts do not build their cars themselves but, in most cases, it's the dads doing it. And we do them very well! It is an obsession with fathers and really should be stopped.

Well, Dad did a great job with that first derby car for John. They painted it to resemble an American flag and John and his father were very proud of their accomplishment when they signed in the day of the derby. The first step was the weigh-in and of course, due to dad's accurate scale, they passed this hurdle with no problem. The scouts lined up and the race began. John's car won heat after heat - and was the first to finish in the final heat! John and his dad were so excited as he received the first place trophy. They beamed with pride standing before the entire Cub Scout pack during the announcement of the Pinewood Derby winners.

Now John was obligated to represent his pack in the regional derby. Unfortunately, Dad had to work that day and Mom was recruited to take John. I couldn't believe the number of boys present at the regional meet! The hall was full of screaming boys waiting in line for hours to race their car. It was extremely difficult keeping John focused on the race because of all of the stimulation. The noise level was almost unbearable. At the end of the day, when John finally raced his car it failed to surpass the others. He barely noticed. He was so ready to get out of there. As we left I felt grateful that we didn't have to move on to the next level of competition. John was just plain glad to be done!

During the summer there was a Cub Scout day camp John was able to attend. Due to the remoteness of the location I was urged to remain on the premises during the time John would be there. The camp director was concerned about John's medical issues, as was the camp nurse. So I volunteered to head up the Arts and Crafts activities for the week John attended the camp program. Again, we had to provide 1:1 coverage for John in order for him to participate safely. My friend, Diane, agreed to take the job and so we began our Cub Scout day camp adventure. She had two children who were able to attend as "tag-alongs" and we all rode the bus together. During this time, John became very close with those two children, and as Diane's and my friendship progressed he came to think of them as surrogate siblings.

Let me tell you, a school bus full of young boys on their way to camp can make for an interesting ride! On the way home they were more subdued, having been so active and out in the fresh air all day. John was fortunate to work with some international counselors from whom he learned much about foreign culture. The camp program included BB gun target practice, as well as archery practice.

I was nervous about both of those activities, but not as concerned as Diane was! When Diane and John arrived at Arts and Crafts the first day of camp, she handed me a BB target sheet with most of the holes in (or near) the bull's eye. Smiling, she said, "Here's John's target practice paper." I thought she was kidding, but sure enough it seemed John was a crack shot with both a BB gun, as well as a bow and arrow! He was so proud of himself - what an experience. It's hard to believe he could focus so well on something of interest to him when much of the time he required constant redirection to the task at hand. It's no surprise that Cub Scout Day Camp is one John's fondest memories of childhood - a time when he was able to bask in the limelight for a change. I would encourage any parents of children with special needs to have their child join the Boy/Girl Scouts of America. The camaraderie shared by those participating in this organization can be an amazing experience!

Twelve

Middle School Madness

Unfortunately, John lost interest in Cub Scouts before he ever got to the Boy Scout level. It was lots of fun when he was young and friendships were easier to facilitate. By the time he reached middle school age he found it even more difficult to keep up with the conversations and social interactions of peers his age. We had been able to help him in this area up until now in a variety of ways. We always had the coolest wading pool and/or sprinkler in the summer that would attract the other kids in the neighborhood. Playing in water always seemed to act like a magnet for any children nearby. We spent countless hours at playgrounds where he could interact with other kids. That sometimes backfired because John craved the motion of the swings and could stay on one forever, if allowed. Most children moved from one activity to another quite frequently, leaving John alone on the swings. We certainly tried everything we could think of to foster friendships. However, John never seemed able to attain friendships on his own. As a matter of fact, I remember an experience from the time when we moved into our new home and I went back to the old house to clean up John's room. While there I discovered something John had written on the wall behind his bed. He penned a cryptic message that went like this: inside a crudely drawn heart were the words "John Walker love friends" and beside it "John Walker hate lonleyness (sic)". My heart broke as I read those words and realized the depth of his emotions. Who knows when he wrote it and what precipitated this action? It was too painful for me to ask him. I often wonder if he shared his angst with the therapist he has seen since late childhood. I certainly was never aware of how much he was suffering.

It's hard to be a friend to someone who doesn't understand the give and take of conversation and often wants everything his way. My friends' children (and John's cousins, too) found it increasingly difficult to spend time with John in public as they grew older. At an age where most teenagers are struggling with their own identities, they are hardly prepared to take on a companion like John. What would their peers think? They must have felt it was too big of a risk that they may alienate the people they were gallantly striving to impress.

About this time John decided it wasn't cool to be seen with his parents. I know this is sort of a right of passage during the teenage years but it really made our lives much more difficult. John refused to go out with us to eat in a restaurant for fear his peers would see him. Going to the mall with John became a long lost memory. So my husband and I would take turns staying at home with John while the other ran errands. Take out meals were the only way we ate from area restaurants. It wasn't worth the power struggle that ensued if we would insist John accompany us anywhere. When we went on vacation we asked John's aunt, uncle and cousin Matt to come along with us. This was an acceptable alternative to John. He enjoyed the time with his favorite cousin and Matt needn't worry about his friends observing his interaction with John. It would be years before John once again tolerated our company in public.

When John was in seventh grade at the private school there was much discussion about the appropriateness of this placement.

While John did fairly well in this environment, he had little chance to interact with children that lived nearby. Most of the children at this school were bused in from far away neighborhoods. And even those kids showed little interest in spending time away from school with John. So it was decided that perhaps the time had come for him to return to public school. We hoped this would give him a better chance to meet friends. Well, this transition was even worse than I could have imagined. I asked that John be placed in seventh grade again so he would not have to make another transition to high school the following year. I felt he would do best with two years of middle school experience before making another move. So, in the fall John began attending a school with several hundred students, rather than fifty students he was accustomed to in his previous school. It must have been overwhelming for him to make such a leap, not to mention he didn't know anyone there. Any of the children he had known from elementary school were now interspersed with the rest from all of the other schools in the city. We tried to make the best of the situation by attempting to prepare him for this huge transition.

Right away it was clear that middle school was a whole different animal from what John was used to. He no longer had the attention small classes afforded him in his prior placement, and his case manager was far from the perfect match for John. She was clueless about how to work with someone like John. Her strategy to force compliance was to scream at him. This was the worst way to reach John. He would immediately shut down when this happened. Her expectations for John were so unreasonable. She thought he should be able to open the padlock on his locker in the midst of the commotion going on in the hallway. When he wasn't able to complete this task she berated him for his inabilities. Then she wrote the combination for the lock on the outside of his locker. Well, that surely wasn't the answer because now anyone could easily open it and help themselves to John's belongings. Trying to reason with this woman was an exercise in futility. She got irritated at each infraction of her ridiculous rules. John's obsessions were interfering with his education and she thought she would have success by demanding him to stop. However, this brought disastrous results. John's psychiatrist explained that attempting to stop someone in the middle of an obsession could cause a violent reaction. John needs a warning before expecting him to end an activity. I use a five minute warning system that is usually successful. My suggestions were often

dismissed by this woman.

About this time, John was watching television and forming his own ideas of what teenagers do. Unfortunately, one of those things he saw portrayed on the screen was the act of mooning someone. (For those who don't remember this faze, mooning involved dropping one's pants and exposing their behind to the bewilderment of all present). Well, John just had to try this one out and he chose what he felt was the perfect opportunity. One day, while

walking in the hall past the teacher's lounge, John stopped and performed his stunt. Now, any other kid would realize that doing this to of a roomful of teachers was probably not a good idea - but not John. He was in it for the shock value and he got what he was looking for, the attention of many teachers at one time. Even after a call home to tell his parents and having to serve detention after school was over, he was no more the wiser. His next infraction was already in the works. The assistant principal at this school was rather effeminate and John inquired one day (in a packed lunchroom) whether he was wearing pink underwear. The kids roared and John was taken to the principal's office where he was given afternoon detention again. There were probably many more blunders committed by him that year that I was never aware of, thank goodness.

Earlier, I alluded to an uncomfortable mismatch between the professional who was overseeing John's program and John. All of the above high jinx didn't help matters any! By the end of the first year at middle school, it was clear John needed to be transferred into a more appropriate learning environment. Mainstreaming doesn't always work for everyone, John included. John was assigned to a new teacher who was much better at figuring out what John could handle and when he was best served in a smaller classroom environment. She approached the challenge of teaching John with a lighthearted sense of humor, making the remaining days in "hormone heaven" bearable for all of us.

1993 Lightning Strikes Twice

The power plant where I worked was bought out by a large company from out of state. After the deal was done, the new owners decided to lay off about half of the work force from the old company. And yes, this included me. Again I left my career job and with it half of my vested retirement and my health insurance that covered my family. Also, to put everything in perspective, I needed shoulder surgery at the time. So here I was out of work, can't get unemployment until I used up my severance pay, and then I could not take a job because of my shoulder surgery. I burned up the severance benefit to pay for the Cobra insurance (a plan for laid off workers). The recovery time after my surgery was long and we had to use up all of our life savings to pay bills. Thank God some of my ex-coworkers were collecting money for me and my family. I will not write their names because there were so many and I would probably miss someone. All I can say is, I love you guys. I can never thank you enough. I'll miss you all for the rest of my life. My wife and I had a talk about this money collecting situation, and she was right about telling these generous people that this would not continue any longer. It had to stop, even though we needed the cash. I had to let go and sever the ties between us. They were still employed at the plant, and I was not. The time had come. This was a sad day in my life. It took a full year to get my new job at another company. By this time we were living on our credit cards and it took several years to dig ourselves out of the hole. The pay at my new job was less than half of what I made at the power plant, but at least we had insurance coverage.

Another traumatic event that occurred during this time was the sudden death of my best friend, Diane. She and I worked together

John enjoys time spent with Diane's son Richard, in Middle School

and also spent a lot of time together outside of school. She was the one who assisted John during his Cub Scout camp experience. Diane's children were like siblings to John because we spent so much time with them. When she died so unexpectedly John had a difficult time accepting

that someone so young could die. He thought people only died when they were very old. Not only did he have trouble with the concept of death but he also had to deal with the loss of his friends, Liz and Richard. Diane's parents took custody of her children after her death and they were unable to understand the depth of the relationship all four of us had shared. They struggled with bringing up two teenagers after not having been responsible for children for a long time. I believe it was too painful for them to see me because, until then, they only had seen me with their daughter. Consequently, the bond we shared with Diane's children was broken and John lost his best friend, Richard. Richard had sort of an odd personality and therefore was not too bothered by John's quirky behavior. He found John's antics humorous, accepting John for who he was and just rolling with the punches. It was very hard for me to see John so unhappy in a situation that we had little control over. We had no choice but to carry on.

John's educational teammet often, planning his next year at the high school. At the end of the year John participated in his middle school graduation ceremony, with his anxious parents in the audience waiting for the other shoe to drop. He surprised all of us by behaving in an absolutely appropriate manner during the graduation exercises and we applauded his newfound maturity. Finally he exited the middle school for the last time, ready for a new adventure.

John decided he wanted to get a job that summer. He noticed his peers had begun to work and he wanted to do the same. We felt he wasn't ready for the responsibility a paying job

John celebrates Middle School graduation with his extremely supportive teacher, Jean Loughan.

required and so we encouraged him to do some volunteer work. He chose to spend time at his favorite record store sorting records. A job coach made this experience possible and John continued working there for several years before the store abruptly went out of business. John showed up to work one day only to find a sign on the door stating the store had closed permanently. This was a devastating blow to John. That summer we tried to fill his time with day trips and other fun activities in an attempt to soothe his loss. Before long it was time to go back to school and begin his new adventure as a high school student.

John, in his element, sorting records at his first job in a record store.

Thirteen

High School Already?

It was so hard to believe John was already old enough to be entering high school but, sure enough, the time had come. Late in the summer John attended a week-long orientation session for incoming freshman. He would come home each day excited about activities he participated in, which included many ice-breakers and trust-building exercises. (He was particularly proud of his prowess at lunch when he ate the most pizza of anyone there!) His special education program provided 1:1 coverage during this time and I felt pretty comfortable with the arrangement. Many people I knew from my job in the school department worked at the high school so I felt relatively sure that I'd know what was going on. John seemed unconcerned about the huge transition he was about to make. I tried very hard to help him choose the same clothing and school supplies his peers had. I felt it was necessary for John to fit into the mainstream as much as possible. Backpack in hand, he was dressed and ready to go right on time that first day. Off he went onto his next adventure.

Arriving at school, I stopped the car near the door leading to the special education classroom, where John was expected to begin his day. As I pulled up to the curb John inquired why we were stopping here. I told him it was the closest door to where he needed to go. He answered indignantly that he wanted to go in the same door "everyone else" did. So I hopped out of my car, went into the special education classroom, and informed the staff someone would have to go to the main entrance to meet John. He was refusing to use a different door than the rest of the student body. It seems no one had ever given much thought to how special education students felt about having a separate entrance into the building. From this point forward all students were dropped off at the main door of the high school. John felt empowered after he initiated change on the very first day of school. He was determined to be treated as a mainstream member of his high school and made sure everyone was aware of his intention!

The school year began with a few obstacles, which were to be expected. Surely John would have some difficulty navigating unknown territory at the same time he was adjusting to his new routine. Most of that first year was devoted to fine tuning his program through trial and error. It was pretty obvious John still needed a huge amount of support. The tricky part was how to provide it without him feeling different. His team came up with some clever strategies to address this challenge. We had spent lots of time discussing what we thought might work for John in high school, however, we really knew very little about what would actually happen. John was pretty much in denial of his disability, which made our job very tricky. After all, hadn't we always told him he could do anything he set out to?

The social ramifications involved in high school life were a real challenge. John tried so hard to be like everyone else but, unfortunately, his judgment was impaired which caused many problems. For instance, one day he noticed that one of his peers had dyed her hair a lovely shade of blue. Remembering a commercial advertisement he had seen recently, John inquired whether she had used Tidy-Bowl (a blue toilet bowl cleaner) in her hair. It was fortunate for him that the student was amused by his question. This was not always the case.

At lunchtime John found the cafeteria a nightmarish assault to his senses. His hypersensitivity to sound, smell, and sight caused him much distress. Being so over stimulated, he most likely would have preferred to escape it somehow. However, this time of the day was probably his best chance to practice peer interactions. Staff working with him tried desperately to facilitate conversation between John and his fellow students. John made certain everyone knew his aversion at being associated with some of the other, more obviously disabled, special education students. It seemed odd to me that he wanted nothing to do with the others when he had so many issues himself. But, be that as it may, it was a choice John made early on. As a matter of fact, years earlier he began to refuse riding to school on the "little yellow bus". John decided to remove himself from any way he could be seem different than the typical high school student. He watched closely, observing the other students' behavior, which often was unacceptable. His struggle to facilitate friendships continued throughout his first year at high school. John couldn't understand why the reactions he received when mimicking his peers weren't always positive. He didn't realize how inappropriate teenagers can be and missed completely the fact that they only did these things behind the teacher's back. Consequently, he often found himself in trouble.

John's freshman year at high school was pretty much a big experiment. Both the staff, as well as John, were never quite sure how things were going to shake down. Some classes were very appropriate for him, while others moved

Art Class—his saving grace.

along too quickly for John's delayed processing abilities. It was clear from the start that his lack of attention was still a big problem. One of the strategies implemented to help John focus better in class was to sketch pictures about what he was learning. This may seem like a distraction to you and I, but for John it really worked. He was able to garner much more information when using this strategy. However, I was shocked when I opened his sex education notebook one day to find drawings showing exactly how closely he listened during this class!

Near the end of John's freshman year his team met to discuss how his program would be set up for the next year. Experiences he had during the first year of high school defined the appropriateness of future educational strategies. John was an intelligent young man and could very well have completed much of the coursework, the question was how to accomplish the task. We discovered that a multimodal approach was most helpful to him. Whenever possible, John's program was adapted to include visual and tactile modes of gathering information, rather than having him rely on auditory information alone. He was much more successful and confident using this approach.

There were times when John wanted to take classes that weren't a good fit for him. For instance, he found it difficult to keep up with the pace of the class during a Spanish course. His processing delay also interfered with his ability to participate in computer classes. It wasn't that he couldn't grasp the material, he just needed to do it at his own pace. With this in mind, his educational team came up with a plan for John's sophomore year.

One of the most valuable components to John's program the following year came in the form of a peer tutor. Early in his sophomore year of high school, John was introduced to another student, Tim, who had volunteered to help him. This was a match made in heaven! John was thrilled to work with someone who was caring and patient, while helping him meet his needs. This new friend made all the difference to John's whole outlook about school. John would come home each day very excited and he'd talk about his friend and their adventures. One time they inadvertently left an area of the school without informing the person who was supervising John. When she finally found them, she berated both of them for this indiscretion. John never forgave that staff member for interfering with his friendship. He refused to be associated with her ever again, having felt so betrayed. I'd like to think that a lesson was learned that day about how to insure John's safety without damaging his struggling self esteem. Thankfully, Tim carried on his friendship with John, and continued to work with him throughout the remainder of high school. John still speaks of this relationship as one of the most positive in his life. To this day John's face will light up when recalling the treasured

Peer buddies made all the difference in John's enjoyment of the high school experience.

time he spent with this friend. We recently watched a video I had never seen before. John had filmed it while he was a student in a media class. He was interviewing people and his friend was one of the lucky people he chose to interview. Tim fought back laughter when answering John's queries. Although the questions were humorous to Tim, John was absolutely serious. You could clearly see the respect Tim felt for John. We all must realize how important respect is to people with autism. It's easy to forget that autistic people have feelings, just like all of us do, even though they seldom show them.

When looking back through John's home/school notebooks I am transported back in time. It was often noted that John showed signs of fatigue by the end of the school day. It must have been so difficult for him to hold it together all day long. When John would get home, he'd immediately head to his room to unwind. We found completing homework assignments in the evening almost impossible.

John's ADHD medication had worn off by then and his frustration was palpable. We were able to make arrangements for John to complete his assignments during study hall, with assistance from the people who had attended class with him and had observed how the lessons were taught. It was important to use the same language the teachers had used during the lesson when doing the homework. John can become easily frustrated when the different words are used for the same meaning. Gone were the endless hours we spent each night attempting the impossible. What a relief for all of us!

When planning John's schedule for his junior year of high school he expressed interest in taking a culinary arts course. This particular school was well known for this program. It seemed like something that John could have success with so we signed him up. Little did we realize how much his food allergies would interfere with this class. John is highly allergic to shellfish, so much so that he gets sick when smelling it cooking, never mind eating it! Very often the menus would include clams or scallops. So we would have to make alternative arrangements for that day. Some of the boys in this class thought it was funny to tease John. They began to routinely pick on him whenever the teacher wasn't looking. We started to see negative changes in John's outlook about school. When questioning him, he reluctantly shared details of this torment. It seems that the boys would grab at his nipples (when I was a child these were called "titty twisters") because they knew it upset him. This childish prank had a huge impact on John. He assumed that these boys thought he was a homosexual because they were doing this to him. No one ever really knows why and how John forms these conclusions. It was hard to get him to understand that the teasing had nothing to do with sexual orientation. I tried to convince him to ignore the boys, explaining it was his extreme reaction they were looking for. We even met with the vice principal about this issue but when the discussion failed to resolve the problem, John ultimately dropped the class in order to escape these students and their insensitivity.

The next hurdle we were presented with was the Junior Prom.

I wondered how John felt when he saw all the hubbub going on around this event. When asked if he would like to attend the prom, he promptly dismissed any interest in it. John had often expressed his sadness about not having a girlfriend. He felt left out when he saw the public displays of affection high school students engage in. I've explained to him that when the time is right, he will find someone to love. I wish there were more we could do for him in this matter. Unfortunately, it's one of those challenges in his life that we are unable to help him with. Lord knows what will happen when, or if, the time comes for John to have a romantic interlude with a woman. We will cross that bridge when we come to it.

John works with cartoonist, Chet.

As John turned sixteen we began to plan for his impending adulthood. A vocational rehabilitation counselor met with him to assess his employment skills. She noticed John's artistic talent and his interest in drawing cartoons. We tried to come up with ways for John to use this natural ability. About this time there was an article in the newspaper about a local man who was a cartoonist. His interview was quite interesting and I thought perhaps John could meet him. The vocational rehabilitation counselor made the contact and found out this man was interested in having John do an internship with him. After the appropriate paperwork was completed we set up a plan for John to meet with this man during his summer break from school. They worked several hours a week together and the cartoonist, Chet, was impressed with John's skills. Chet would draw his cartoons in pencil and John would ink over them. Then the pencil lines would be erased and shading added. I never realized all that went into producing a cartoon strip. John was a quick study and before long the cartoonist was giving John more and more responsibilities. At the end of the internship he asked John to work for him from our home. John was thrilled with his offer and quickly accepted! John continued his cartoon work for Chet from our home. Chet was amazed at how well John had picked up the necessary skills. After a couple of years working together Chet reluctantly informed John that he could no longer afford the luxury of an assistant. It was difficult for John to accept the news but he seemed to understand Chet's dilemma. They have maintained a friendship up to this time. John will occasionally have contact with Chet and is always thrilled to show him his latest drawings. And Chet enjoys looking at John's work, always giving him affirmation of his talent.

You Don't Know!

One day my son, John, came in, sat down next to me in my chair, and asked me why his best friend, Thomas, was able to have a driver's license and he was not. Oh my, what was I supposed to tell him. He was so serious and sad. It really broke my heart, I did not know what to say right at that time. It totally took me by surprise! I thought, and Oh my God, remembered when I was his age what a big deal it was for me to drive. It was the biggest, most important thing in any young man's life at this age. What was I to do? What would I tell him? What was a dad to say? I was crushed. I fought back tears and told him it was because of his seizure disorder that he couldn't drive. How would he feel if he had a seizure and crashed into someone, hurting them? As usual, he said that would not be good. Because of his feelings for other people I knew he would be okay with this. God love him, he is such a good and caring person. (Can you believe it?) He totally accepted this as a mature adult should have and I was so proud of him.

Fourteen

Guardianship

As John's eighteenth birthday loomed in the distance, we began to realize we would need to start thinking about guardianship of him. It was clear to us that, although John made huge gains over the years, he was still lacking the judgment necessary to ensure his safety. I attended a workshop covering legal issues parents needs to consider as their child with a disability reaches adulthood. One of the most difficult decisions we had to make was whether to pursue guardianship of our adult son. We were quite sure John needed our help, although he would most likely disagree with us about that!

We met with an attorney to begin the legal procedure. He informed us that it is difficult to prove a person so incapacitated they would require a guardian. He was concerned that John's intelligence, combined with his verbal ability, would prevent us from being appointed his guardians. But, feeling it was absolutely necessary, we went ahead and filed the paperwork with the county probate court. We were told to collect anecdotal evidence of John's inability to function independently. From this point forward, we were told to keep a journal chronicling times John was a danger to himself or others. Entries included the many times John stepped out into traffic without looking first; another time when he left toast in the toaster that got stuck and burned (filling the house with smoke while he rocked in a chair oblivious to it); and purchasing an item at the store without collecting the change due him. During each of these incidents I was forced to rescue John.

The entire court procedure was very traumatic. First, a sheriff appeared at our door to serve us the papers. Next, an attorney was appointed to represent John in court. After this lawyer visited with John, he informed me he would not fight the guardianship order because he agreed with us that John was unable to care for himself. One day we had to take John with us to a meeting with our attorney. Up until that time our attorney had expressed concern that the motion for guardianship would be denied. However, after watching John's actions in his office that day, the lawyer changed his mind and told us we had nothing to worry about!

The dreaded day finally arrived and we drove up the driveway to the courthouse. John knew why we were going to court that day, but he remained unconvinced he needed our help when he was an adult. Everything seemed surreal as we entered the courthouse and first were required to walk through a metal detector. John seemed to revel in this experience. His attorney met us in the foyer. He told us that our attorney had been delayed in another courtroom, causing us to wait for his arrival before the proceeding could begin. While we waited, John's attorney tried to convince him to sign the paperwork voluntarily. No dice! John wanted his day in court and so we waited. The bailiff took John on a tour of the courthouse to try and pass the time. When John saw the video cameras in the courtroom he asked to see Judge Judy. (A judge on a popular TV show). Everyone chuckled but, sure enough, the judge presiding over our case was a female! When our attorney arrived, we entered the courtroom. John and his attorney were seated opposite us. After swearing to tell the truth (the whole truth), the proceedings began. I felt I was watching a television show, or having a bad dream, instead of really having this experience. Right away. I was called as a witness and asked to prove my case. Every time I opened my mouth to read and then explain the incidents written in my journal, John would yell out, "That's a lie!" His actions came as a total shock to me. As I returned to my seat, I turned to my attorney and said, "I can't believe he said that!" He replied, "Who do you think she will believe?" I took a deep breath as John was sworn in. He sat in the witness stand proudly. Every question the judge asked him was answered with conviction. When asked whether he had a job, John answered, "Not yet." The judge inquired how he would pay his bills. John answered by rattling off a multitude of credit cards he would use. Every word out of this mouth dug him in deeper. We left the courtroom convinced we had proved our case!

That awful day remains imprinted in my mind as the most difficult and devastating I have experienced in parenthood. After all the times I had assured John "You can do it", I was forced to stand before him and say, "You can't do it". I absolutely feel the court system is flawed and a parent should never have to be put in this place. I fully understand people have abused their guardianship power, but it seems a travesty to force parents into the situation we endured when we were only trying to protect our child from harm.

My biggest fear during the guardianship court case was that John would get on the stand and make a fool of himself and be humiliated. I don't think I could handle this. Thank Goodness the attorneys did a great job with the questions. The questions I felt really nailed it were: "John, what do the colors of a traffic light mean?" John responded immediately by saying, "The red light mean to stop and the green light means to go, but I don't know what the yellow light means." And then John was asked, "If you bought something that cost 75 cents and you had only a one dollar bill, how much change should you get back?" John looked a little confused and then said, "I think maybe a few quarters." The judge said thank you and dismissed us. John and I drew a large sigh of relief.

At that point I knew it would be alright.

Once guardianship was granted, our next nightmare began. We were required to keep track of every penny John had. At the end of the year we had to file paperwork accounting for every penny he had. I would spend hours collecting and recording the information on the forms provided. At 18 John became eligible for assistance from both federal and state agencies. However, he got so little money to spend on his daily needs that we always had to give him more cash to make it through until he received his next payment. It seemed ridiculous to go through all of the accounting for money that came in and went out again before the month was over. I petitioned the court to end this excessive accounting of funds and, thankfully, the court agreed with me and granted the motion. We still have to complete a yearly report on John's well-being, but that pales in comparison to the original paperwork.

I hope I haven't discouraged parents from seeking guardianship - that's not my intent. I just feel strongly that people should be prepared for the emotional impact this procedure brings. In this time of many new privacy laws, it is even more important to be appointed guardian of your child if they are unable to function independently. I must provide proof of guardianship before being allowed to obtain medical information, insurance information, or to help assure John's medical care is appropriate. We have never regretted our decision to become John's legal guardians, and feel it helps us keep John safe and well taken care of. This is definitely an individual decision for each family to make, based on their child's needs. One of the biggest concerns we had was that without legal guardianship, John could decide to leave home totally unprepared to function out in the world and we would have no right to challenge his actions. That scared the daylights out of us, so we made sure the appropriate papers were in order well before his eighteenth birthday. Although the process was traumatic, we can sleep at night knowing John is safe and sound.

Fifteen

Graduation Looms

H aving just recovered from the whole guardianship experience, we braced ourselves for the next huge transition in John's life - high school graduation. As most of you know, the senior year of high school is a flurry of activity that culminates on graduation day. John and I began this journey with a visit to a photographer for his yearbook picture. John was never very cooperative when having a formal picture taken - he just tried way too hard. The fake, plastered-on smile has been our nemesis throughout years of school pictures. However, it was amazing to see how differently John approached this photo opportunity. I think that because he so desperately wanted to fit in with his peers (his desire to appear "like everyone else" in the yearbook) gave him the momentum to make it through this difficult experience. I helped John carefully choose the clothing that we felt would be the most appropriate for this big day. He had many shots taken in a variety of dress and poses. The photographer had a way about her that made John feel comfortable and relaxed right away. The resulting portfolio of prints were incredible. Not to sound too much like a proud mom or anything, but our handsome son looked fabulous! We chose one of the more formal of shots to go into the yearbook. John wore a green button-down shirt, not really what he would have worn everyday, but its' color perfectly complimented his beautiful red hair. We thought it would be a better choice for the yearbook than the more informal shots where John wore jeans, tee shirt and baseball cap (more his normal attire). After all, one only has the opportunity to appear as a senior in the yearbook once so you might just as well give it your best shot (no pun intended!).

Upon completing that first rite of passage as a senior in high school, John was propelled into an emotional roller coaster of a senior year. He was experiencing the myriad of emotions that most high

school seniors do, but for John these feelings were magnified many times over. People with autism struggle with emotionally charged situations. Thank Goodness John had the benefit of a wonderful psychologist that he had been seeing since he was about twelve years old, who was trained to work with children who have speech and language concerns. She was John's lifeline during this tumultuous time.

While most of his peers were applying to colleges, John also was intensely interested in higher education. However, the reason he gave to pursue college was a desire to live in a dorm, far away from parents, where he could party. His limited exposure to college culture consisted of movie footage chronicling wild drinking parties in fraternities. Being easily convinced, John desired this so-called good life. When we pulled him back into the reality of college coursework and the studying and effort involved, he quickly lost interest. At this point in his life, John reached his saturation point as far as academics were concerned. We struggled to keep him focused enough to complete the schoolwork necessary for graduation. Although John had been "mainstreamed" into high school classes, the school's expectations were relaxed enough to acknowledge his disability. I contend that if a student is not able to adequately complete the mandatory coursework guidelines for graduation, they should not receive the same diploma those able to do. To me it seems a travesty to award all graduates in the same manner. Presenting a high school diploma to an employer presents certain expectations that some people with a disability cannot meet. I'm not sure what the answer to this dilemma is, but it probably should be addressed in order to prevent this problem. I know how important belonging to the group is, but perhaps a certificate of completion housed in the same case as a diploma would work. No one would be the wiser at the graduation ceremony and it would avoid setting someone up to expectations they are unable to meet.

Hearing all the chatter among his peers about what lay ahead was a huge distraction for John. However, before we knew it the graduation planning was in full swing. John was pulled into a whirlwind of activities wrapping up his high school experience. He opted to bypass the senior prom but looked forward to graduation night and the chemical-free party that followed the ceremony.

At this time I was busy with my own planning for a party to commemorate this momentous occasion. The enormous amount of effort involved in putting together such a large event presented a much needed diversion from all that was happening. Had I been more aware of the changes occurring daily, I think I would have fallen apart completely! We decided to include all of the people who were responsible for John reaching this goal to this party. John was very much a part of putting together the guest list. He had definite ideas about who should and should not be invited to his graduation party. In the end we came up with a total of nearly fifty invitees, all of whom had impacted John in one way or another along the road to graduation. These included teachers, speech and language therapists, occupational therapists, his adapted physical education teacher, and special education paraprofessionals, etc. Each played an important role in the successful outcome we were about to celebrate.

While I was busy with my event planning, John was fully immersed in the activity leading up to graduation day. He reluctantly spent grueling hours practicing marching into the auditorium with his fellow graduates. He reveled in the more social aspects, such as signing yearbooks. I do believe John felt very much a part of the festivities, perhaps this was the first time he truly felt a member of his class.

When graduation night arrived, we sat nervously in the audience awaiting John's entrance into the auditorium. It was a pleasant surprise when we saw John was all business, marching among his peers to his seat. His face was etched with emotion as he patiently listened to the many speakers at the podium. Finally, the moment we had been waiting so many years for, arrived. John's name was called to receive his diploma and dutifully he rose to the occasion. With a 10,000 megawatt smile, John approached the podium amid the cheers from his proud contingent of supporters. It is said a picture is worth a thousand words, and the photo snapped at this time surely conveys that. We had not seen John more happy in his life than he was at this moment. He basked in the glory of achieving a lifetime goal. We must have taken a hundred pictures to capitalize on the memory we had waited so long for.

Graduation

I did not want to videotape this event because I told my wife I wanted to just be a regular parent watching the whole event happen. Well, it did, and I have to say I was totally impressed with the young girl who was seated next to John. She apparently was instructed to help John with the whole proceedings, because she helped him by telling him when to stand, sit, or do anything. Well, I would like to thank her and her parents for her cooperation and help with our son, John. It surely did distract her from her own graduation experience. And we thank her, whoever she was. We love you, you're the best!

Let me tell you, I sat at John's graduation totally helpless and watch my son trying so hard to stay on task and pay attention to what was going on. He was so proud of his class and all of the proceedings that were happening that night. The strain on his face was so evident, I was almost in tears, watching him. I took a deep breath and regained my composure, thank goodness. We have a picture we took that shows what it was like. Well, he did great walking up and getting his diploma, thanks to that girl.

After the tossing of caps and rounds of high fives, we were reunited with our son, who appeared to have grown up in a moment's time. He came home long enough for a quick family celebration, then changed into jeans and a tee shirt. He was ready to party the night away with his classmates! We had asked a respite care provider to accompany John to this all-night party and, thankfully, he obliged. Fortunately his care provider was merely a bit older than John so he fit right in with the high school crowd.

Somewhere near dawn we received a call from John requesting a ride home. He had reached his saturation point, as the emotions of the past 24 hours caught up with him. I quickly drove to the destination point to collect one exhausted and relieved eighteen year old! Thus concluded John's public school experience, spanning the last fourteen years

As I said earlier in the book, John and I invited many of the people responsible for his school successes to celebrate his graduation with our family. After giving John time to recover from the all night party, we gathered our guests into a large rented room for a final celebration. Months of planning insured every detail had been tended to. The tables were draped with the maroon and gold school colors, with confetti and balloons completing the decorations. I had carefully compiled photographs chronicling John's journey through school and assembled a huge poster, using a photo of him in his cap and gown as the centerpiece. Looking at the finished product, I was pulled back in time to that first day at PEEP. There stood John proudly waving to me from the doorway of the little yellow bus on his first day of school. Then, in chronological order, were his yearly school pictures. School picture day was never easy and the resulting portrait was often less than impressive. But John was John - in all his glory! I left room on this huge poster for guests to write comments and sign their names when they entered the room. A maroon-draped graduate stood on top of the cake I had decorated, overlooking the festivities.

Guests filed in to the music John had carefully chosen for this day. He was extremely proud as he greeted each guest, and the party began. We feasted and visited, enjoying one another's company. Then came the moment that surprised us all . . . John assembled and then introduced each attendee who impacted his education. He not only recognized them by name, he spoke briefly of their role in his life. We videotaped the entire event and often look back in amazement at how appropriately he did this. Flash bulbs popped as guests snapped pictures of John surrounded by all of the wonderfully patient people who guided him through to this outcome. Their smiles couldn't have been any wider. It was a moment in time we'll never forget. As the party wound down, goodbyes were said and we took a deep breath. This part of our journey had ended and we braced ourselves for a new beginning. John's life as an adult was about to unfold before us.

John thanks some of those responsible for helping him during his school years, on the road to graduation. Left to right: Maryann, Karen, Kathy, Maria, Deb, Sue, Lynn and Claire.

Sixteen

Transition

In our local school system, special education students graduate with their class and then complete a transition period before they turn 21 years old, at which time they enter the adult system. In preparation for writing this chapter in John's life, I read through the notebooks that were used at this time to communicate with those who were working with John. Throughout his school career, we were fortunate to have many talented and patient people impact John's life in a positive way. It was apparent that the person working directly with John (usually a paraprofessional) was the most important cog in the wheel. The special education team made decisions about his program, and then continually checked to be sure the plans were being adhered to. When the program moved out of the school environment, into the community, we found holding staff accountable (with spotty supervision, at best) a challenge. I began to realize that now, more than ever, the direct care person would make or break the program. They could follow the carefully planned daily schedule or choose to deviate from it. Unfortunately, John's first care provider chose the latter.

The two years of transition from school to adult life became more of a headache than I could ever have imagined. It seemed I had to continually investigate what was happening and then try to correct the problems that were occurring. Each day brought a new challenge. I had to be at my job early in the morning, so John's day began when the care provider arrived at our house. She was responsible for getting John ready to begin his day.

From the start this person was often late getting to our house, which meant I would also be late to work. Once she did arrive, she was left to oversee John's morning routine. John, never being a morning person, gave her a run for her money. To make things easier for both of them, I instituted a checklist system for John to follow. He would check off each of the steps necessary to get ready for the day as he completed them. This was the first of many times it became my responsibility to find ways around obstacles that cropped up during transition time.

I was the parent who attended planning meetings and dealt with day-to-day issues. When it came time to write about this, I read the communication books out loud to John's dad. He was floored by the conflict I endured during this time. He couldn't believe the kinds of problems brought up daily.

John's educational team had a very specific plan mapped out so he could practice life skills in the community. He was supposed to do his laundry, learn how to cook and clean up afterward, and work on various other skills he would need in order to be as independent as possible. It was essential he receive adequate supervision while honing these skills, both for his safety, as well as completing the tasks efficiently.

There was an apartment downtown that the area agency used as a respite site for parents of children who have disabilities to use when they needed an escape from life's challenge. It was usually available on weekdays, so the agency offered its' use to the school department for their transition program. John enjoyed shopping for the groceries he would need to cook a meal in the apartment. He would prepare the food and then clean up after himself. He beamed with pride as he later recounted his success! However, upon questioning John about the remainder of his day, he might relay that he and his aide watched television all afternoon. John already knew how to watch television! He desperately needed to learn how to relate to others in the community. Again, it was up to me to report this and help find a solution to the problem.

One day John came home thrilled to show me a pile of "junk" he had accumulated over the course of the day. It seems he was busy that day going through the castaway belongings that city residents had put on the curb for the public works department to pick up. I was less than impressed with how John had spent his day. It seems the care provider had her own pick of "treasures" that day. One item was a large rug she had John help her put into her car which they then took to her house miles away! Needless to say, this incident prompted yet another call to her supervisor, where I recounted my dismay that such an activity would be included in John's transition program.

I found myself constantly reporting inappropriate use of John's time, not to mention how John's safety often was being breached. She even asked John to sit in her vehicle while she attended meetings at her childrens' schools. There was no end to the poor choices she made, day after day.

I would guess it must have been difficult to find a replacement for this person, because otherwise there is no explanation why this was allowed to continue. Accountability seemed a foreign concept for this program's employees. I never gave up trying - I kept thinking things would get better and requested a new individual work with John the following year.

Unfortunately, my pleas fell on deaf ears and we began the second year with the same person. She assured me she would try harder to meet John's needs. I made sure there was a busy schedule of activities each day and checked with John about how each day went. He would be distressed if I showed disappointment in how his aide carried out her job. There was some sort of bond they had and he accepted what happened because he didn't know any better.

John was obsessed with the Spanish language at this time so we enrolled him in an independent study Spanish course at the local university. He could work at his own pace, using a computer in the Spanish lab to follow the lessons. There was a coffee hour each week, where students would practice their use of Spanish. John loved this activity and looked forward to each meeting. This coffee hour was one of the most positive interactions John probably had during his time in the community.

John also loves music and so we looked into having John access the university's radio station. He did visit a few times, but was disappointed to find that most of the activity there occurred in the evening or on weekends, times not covered under his transition program. Therefore, we did not have anyone to supervise him at the radio station. In order to have John appear more independent, we have refrained from being the ones to provide supervision when John is out in the community.

In May of 1999, we moved away from the only home John ever knew. We had brought him home from the hospital to the house that we had bought shortly after our marriage. For the next twenty years we enjoyed many good times in that home. But we were fortunate to find a new home better suited to all of our needs.

The Big Move

This day was so exciting, yet so stressful, for both me and my wife because of all the memories we were about to leave behind in that old place. It was so hard for us. But for John, it was even harder. He was so happy to get a room that was at least three times larger than his old room. It was hard for him to accept he was not at home any more. He said, "What am I going to do without my room?" I drew a heavy breath and said, "John, our old house and your old room have become too small for us so we have to move to a bigger place so everything could be better." He accepted that, but it was still hard for him. My wife and I had a big adjustment, as well. Ironically, looking back at it now, I think that it was harder for us than it was for our son. Moving day came and John and his Uncle Jeff took on the task of moving his record collection. John was very careful to keep each record in the order he categorized them. It took a very long time for the two of them to complete this monumental task, but they eventually achieved their goal. The move was a big transition for John. We were so busy at the time we hardly noticed his anxiety surrounding the event. We now realize what a hard thing it was for him to give up what he knew for the unknown. Today he'll tell you that he loves his new room but he still misses the old house and all of the memories we made there.

Toward the end of John's second transition year, we began to investigate arrangements for when he moved from being entitled to special education programming on into the adult care system. John, his father, and I attended a vendor fair that was organized by the area agency which would provide his adult care. Many different vendor agencies offering day programs for adults had set up booths where we could view their brochures and speak with them individually. It was overwhelming to try and choose which agency would do the best job servicing John's needs. They all talked a good talk, so we investigated further by asking other families about their experiences.

We finally made a choice, based on the positive feedback we received from families using their services. As we wrapped up the transition segment of John's life (not a moment too soon) we set out to plan activities John would pursue during his day program. The vendor agency we chose met with the area agency to discuss details of funding, etc. Then we attended a formal meeting to make decisions about how to proceed into the next chapter of John's life, the adult care system.

Seventeen

Adult Care System

After years of entitled special education, which is mandated for children ages 3 - 21, at twenty one years of age John entered the adult system and all of its intricacies. In our state, services for adults who have developmental disabilities are overseen by area agencies. We had been working in conjunction with our area agency staff since John began the transition process at the age of sixteen. Therefore, he was included in the budgeted funding when he turned 21. We were thrilled to find that he had enough money set aside to fund thirty hours of programming a week. How this would be used was up to us! John was very vocal about what kinds of activities he was interested in. He also was adamant he wanted to have a job, "just like everyone else".

Armed with this information, John's individual service program team set out to come up with a plan for a successful day program. It was determined early on that John would be best served by an individual care provider so finding the right one was the first order of business. The team felt it would be helpful to have a male provide the supervision and carry out the plan. I was very nervous about allowing a complete stranger to have sole responsibility for John's safety and happiness for thirty hours a week. The vendor agency sought to soothe my fears by assuring me that they only hired "highly qualified staff that were trained to attend to each individual client's needs". I was a hard sell but I reluctantly put my faith into their hands.

Before we knew it the day came to meet the new care provider, someone the agency highly recommended. We were told he had a long history working in the disability field. We arranged for him to come to the house so he could meet John, his dad and I. We filled him in about our medical concerns and what expectations we had for his time with John.

The first day of program, John and I met "Bill" (a fictitious name) at our door. We had arranged to have their day begin at 8:00 a.m., when I would be leaving for work during the school year. Thankfully, I was on vacation for the summer, so I was available to help with John's transition into this program. We had come up with a checklist of things John needed to do in order to begin his day. It has always been extremely helpful for John to have visual, as well as auditory, directions. I would busy myself with chores while John, with Bill's assistance, completed the steps from his list.

Bill was comfortable with us almost immediately - so comfortable that he began to make his tea at our house each morning, sipping contentedly away while John got ready. Initially I wasn't concerned because they left for their program day reasonably early in the morning. However, as the summer wore on it seemed they were stretching the time out so they weren't leaving until mid-morning, when John's program activities were intended to begin by nine o'clock. I expressed my concern about this, and for awhile it seemed to improve. I returned to work at the end of the summer, when Bill and I began to communicate via a notebook. In the mornings I was usually rushing off to work so it was hard to communicate much then. It was also difficult to have a conversation in front of John without him becoming anxious. Bill dropped John off at the school where I worked at the end of their day. I was still working at the time, so John would go to the staff room and read his newspaper while he waited for me. The communication notebook seemed to work well, until John began to share tidbits about his day that weren't included in the notebook. One such activity John mentioned was shopping at a health food store on a regular basis. I was fairly certain that my "junk food junkie" of a son was not requesting this errand be included in his day!

On the very first day I had off from school I felt inclined to visit a neighbor while John and Bill completed their morning routine, so as to not interrupt their routine. Imagine my surprise when I returned home to find them still there. Even more astonishing was the scene I walked in on. John sat in front of the television while Bill sorted family photographs on my kitchen table. He quickly explained to me that he was working on a project (like I would accept this as an appropriate use of John's time). As I said earlier, it was really difficult to discuss anything in front of John without him becoming defensive. He would have been happy to sit glued to the television all day long, rather than go out into the community where he knew there were many expectations he would have to deal with. I would write in the notebook about my displeasure, but not much changed. One day Bill and John went to the local mall and I received a frantic call from Bill telling me that John was missing. Before I could make arrangements to leave work and help search for John, I got a call saying a mall security guard had reunited him with his care provider. This incident prompted yet another meeting to discuss John's safety.

Before long it was summer again and Bill routinely did not show up for work in the morning. I would then call the agency, who would send a replacement to pick up John for the day. I found out that some days John would just sit in the office at the agency, like he was being babysat. This again was unacceptable in both John's and my eyes. During this time John was supposed to be seeking employment, but not much was happening there either. After a week of being absent without calling his employer, Bill was terminated. A message was left on his answering machine by the agency, but two weeks later he suddenly showed up one morning and appeared oblivious to everything. I sent him off for the agency to deal with. What an experience we had with our very first person! We could only hope that the new person hired to work with John would be a huge improvement over what we previously had experienced.

Eighteen

Stolen Innocence

At the risk of scaring the pants off any reader who has a child with autism, I feel compelled to share the story of the most deceptive care provider John has ever had. It has taken a very long time to bolster my courage enough to write about this most disturbing experience. After our disappointment with the way the first year of John's day program had shaken down, we were anxiously awaiting a much more suitable care provider for John. Instead, our world was about to be turned upside down.

For a period of time after Bill's departure, the vendor agency used a variety of people to fill in until a permanent employee was hired to work with John. The agency's job developer even filled in and worked well with John, although my hope that he could procure employment for our son never reached fruition. After about a month, or more, of waiting for a return to routine we finally were introduced to a young man close to John's age. We interviewed him and found out that, although he was in his early twenties, he had been married and had a son and then was divorced. Later we would discover that he was living with a woman who was pregnant with his child. While I try not to obsess on what happens outside of the care provider's time with John, I have to admit this information concerned me!

107

"Jim", as I'll call him, was a master of deception. He and John hit it off immediately and appeared to enjoy each other's company. I believe John thought of this person as his friend and confided his deepest feelings to him. The first note Jim wrote into John's communication book should have warned me of his immaturity. He answered my home phone (the call was from my doctor, so he wrote the appointment information down) and he explained he had paged his brother and left our number to receive a call back. I just couldn't believe the gall of someone to answer my personal phone and to give my number out for him to receive a call! Right away we had another negative incident with Jim. It seems he and John were visiting a large warehouse store (John would later reveal that Jim was looking for a bicycle to buy for his son) when Jim showed his poor judgment by attempting to use an exercise machine on display. The equipment had not been assembled for public use and one of the pieces became dislodged, striking Jim's face hard enough to break his nose. Now, imagine John's anxiety when the person charged with his safety stood before him bleeding profusely from his nose. John told us later that he went to the service desk to get help for Jim. At this time the agency was called and promptly sent another employee over to rescue John. That person then took John to the hospital so he could see that Jim was going to be okay.

After a couple of days recovery time, Jim returned to work. The next red flag appeared only a week later, when Jim wrote that he had taken John to his house. An inspector from the state had come that day in regard to another client Jim was being paid to provide housing and care for. John ate lunch while they tended to their business and then John watched a movie there. I remember constantly calling John's case manager to complain about inappropriate use of John's time and to report safety concerns, as well. This conversation fell upon deaf ears because the case manager was under Jim's spell and refused to agree there were any problems. He was a real charmer to the ladies but I saw through him. I asked him time and time again to use better judgment, even comparing his work with John to what he would expect from a day care provider for his own son. It just seemed to get worse, instead of better. One day John came home reeking of cigar smoke. I was appalled, John has asthma and should never be around any kind of smoke. John shared that Jim was smoking a cigar in the cab of his truck while driving him around! I made a big stink (no pun intended) about this threat to John's health, but again Jim got away with only a slap on the wrist. We went on like this for a couple of months, the pattern of my complaints being disregarded as trivial continued until it culminated on the worst day of my life.

I was at work one December day, three months into Jim's tenure with John, when I received an urgent phone call. The person on the line introduced herself as an investigator for the state who wanted to interview John about his contact with Jim. It seems another client had recently disclosed inappropriate, dangerous activity while under Jim's supervision. Therefore, an investigation was launched, and the remaining clients he had worked with were being questioned. The investigator wanted to schedule an appointment to talk with John. I suggested an upcoming Monday when my husband and I would be home from work, due to a holiday. We wanted to be there for John but she immediately responded that she needed to talk to John alone - "that's the way it works", she said. I reminded her that John's dad and I were his legal guardians and would only allow an interview where we were present. She reluctantly set up the appointment and thankfully, we didn't have much time to think about it before she came to our house to see John. Our house is situated in such a way that the kitchen and living room are one large area. I set them up at the kitchen table and my husband and I took our places in living room chairs facing away from the kitchen. From this position we could hear the conversation while appearing to watch television. What we heard was so shocking that it was hard to believe. Evidently, Jim had been taking the liberty to allow John to have experiences he never would have had otherwise. John explained that Jim told him not to take his medication on Fridays so they could "party" without John getting sick. John knew he should never drink alcohol or take any drugs because he took medication that would probably interact negatively with them. John revealed they spent Fridays at Jim's friend's house in another city, where they would drink, smoke pot, and watch pornographic movies. Even more disturbing was John's statement "Jim said he was going to bring girls so we could have a gangbang and I would lose my virginity, but every time, there were no girls there". Thank God for that! Al and I sat through this devastating dialogue, unable to let on we were listening. More than an hour later, the investigator left. She said we would receive a report when she was done processing the information.

Unbeknownst to us, she spoke with John again at the area agency a couple of weeks later. At that time she reported John "changed his story" and therefore was an unreliable witness. We are sure the information John gave had merit. He had way too many details to have made it up. When the report came in the mail, I disagreed with the investigator that John's account was unreliable and appealed the findings. Unfortunately, the report was allowed to stand. I'm not sure what punishment Jim received, but I truly believe that what goes around, comes around and he will have his judgment day. Even after all of the gory details were recounted by John, Jim continued to deny them. He said John was lying, but we know full well that if nothing happened, John would never have had so many details. Jim explained that he only wanted to be a friend to John by doing "man things" with him. A true "friend" would never take advantage the way he did. I will be forever thankful that Jim was found out before anything else could happen to John.

Jim had been fired immediately after the allegations were brought forth. John spent a lot of time agonizing over the fact that Jim had lost his job when he had family obligations. We reminded John many times that Jim was grossly inappropriate and used horribly poor judgment, therefore it was his own fault he was unemployed. John's therapist, his father, and I, were finally able to convince John he was not at fault. This whole experience damaged John in so many ways. He will still recount details of what happened during that time, dredging up feelings we hoped had been forgotten long ago. I lose sleep wondering about what happened. We will probably never know exactly what transpired and I am finally able to come to a point where I don't blame myself for allowing this to happen.

At any rate, we came out of this experience irrevocably broken. We will never be able to entirely trust anyone again. It's my hope that no one ever has to go through anything like this ever again. However, I also know there are predators lurking wherever they can find innocent victims. Hopefully, this story will make you, as a reader, more aware and you'll be able to protect your loved ones. I can only wish this entire incident had never happened to our family.

Unbelievable

My wife and I were so upset and angry we didn't know what to do. I was so mad that I would have probably beat this young man to near death if left alone with him anywhere. Thank God we never saw him again. I asked my son to tell me the truth and, as usual, he did. When I asked what these movies were, he told me not only the name of them, but what was in them and that he rented them at our local movie rental store. So I went down to the video store and, for the first time ever, I went into the adult entertainment room in the back of the store. I was totally angered by what I found. I had no problem finding the exact movie John was talking about. I now knew our son was telling my wife and I the truth.

Nineteen

Onward and Upward

After our first two less-than-impressive to downright dangerous encounters with care providers, we were shell-shocked and found it quite impossible to trust anyone with the care of John. However, it was in John's best interest to spend time outside of our home, in the community he was part of. So, we reluctantly trudged on and were introduced to another "carefully chosen" care provider. I have decided not to elaborate on each individual we have entrusted our son's care to over the past seven years because there have been so many that I could write an entire book on just that topic alone.

We have been fortunate to have some excellent staff work with John after the dismal beginning of adult day program services. When I am confident the person is giving John the appropriate respect and attention, I make sure they know how much they are appreciated. It also works in the reverse, when I notice inconsistencies, I address the problem immediately. I no longer am put off by pleas of "wait it out - things will get better", or the promise that the person has been reprimanded and has assured us they will change their ways. John has been through too much to take any more chances. One very young care provider left John at the gym while he went off to get a sandwich and gas up his car. He was unfortunate enough to be caught in the act by his supervisor and was immediately terminated. This is exactly how any infractions should be handled, in my opinion. There is no room for error when entrusted with our most vulnerable individuals. We've seen the gamut of staff, from people who seem to be on another planet, those who show up late each day, some who can't speak our language well enough to be understood, to the truly dedicated, competent professionals we're blessed to know.

It is most important that John be comfortable with whom he spends his days. He is usually a pretty good judge of character and if he seems the slightest bit hesitant to work with someone, I thoroughly investigate the reason he feels this way. He has learned from past mistakes that all people are not worthy of his trust. And John now understands the role of his provider is to keep him safe, not to be his friend. He has had some wonderful interactions with qualified staff who are able to achieve overseeing a successful day program while also enjoying John's company.

When care providers are compensated more appropriately for the monumental responsibility they're given, I think we'll see a change in the quality of care provided. These people are expected to function as the direct link between the family and agency, often without much support or training. I believe that explains why John has had almost twenty caregivers move in and out of his life over the past seven years. For someone who struggles with change and personal interaction, this seems a travesty of justice. However, we have little control over how long people stay on the job. I have learned to take one day at a time and treasure the moments John spends with competent and caring staff. In conclusion, I would like to impress upon all parents to follow your instincts about your child's care - never doubt your gut feelings. It could save your son or daughter from irreversible harm.

Twenty

Our Story Continues

In the previous chapters I have failed to mention John's success in the working world. To this date, he has been employed with the same corporation for five years. From the beginning we realized John would need much support to be able to work. His care provider also serves as his job coach for the two hours each day he spends at work. They are responsible only to ensure John's safety and redirect him when necessary. His supervisor assigns duties to John and is the person he looks to for answers to any questions he may have about the assignment. Through trial and error, John found that having written directions for what is expected of him works the best.

When given adequate support, John is extremely task-driven. It is sometimes necessary to redirect John when he veers off his assignment, becoming distracted by outside stimulation. When John began his job, his duties were mostly janitorial. He never particularly cared for the bathroom cleaning assignment, but he stoically completed the chore each day. He would go through his list of jobs and ask his supervisor what to do if he finished all his work before time to punch out. John has repeatedly asked to be relieved of his bathroom cleaning duty. At first, he was told that was part of his job and he would have to do it or find another job. He accepted this for several years until one day when he was called into the personnel office and was told he no longer would clean toilets. John was so excited to be relieved of that chore and quickly was given lots of different job assignments. He now is much more cheerful about going to work and considers his change in duties as a promotion.

Unfortunately, recently the person who was cleaning the bathrooms at work was absent and John was told to do it. Well, he got very upset and thought he had reverted back to the old days of cleaning toilets. With encouragement, John spoke with his boss about his disappointment (in John's literal world, he said he felt like he had climbed the ladder and now was falling back down it). When it was explained that the change would be temporary he quickly let the incident go.

During the five years John has been employed with the same company, he has made great strides in the work environment. This has carried over with his increased ability to interact with others. I wish I could say John has made friends he would see outside of work, but this is not the case. John is proud to speak about his co-workers, who he considers his friends. Who am I to think otherwise? He has worked with some of the same people for five years so they are a very important part of his life. John recently was presented with a pin and clock, honoring his five year anniversary with the company. The smile on John's face when he came home with his reward was priceless! Every other week he comes home with his paycheck, eagerly awaiting a ride to the bank to cash it. The money he receives is secondary to what working does for his self-esteem and feeling of acceptance by society. I couldn't ask for more than to see John, so happy and fulfilled because of his job.

My only wish is that he feel the same satisfaction outside of his employment. It breaks my heart to hear him speak of how lonely he is. John craves a social life that includes friends to do things with, and most importantly, someone to love. He often laments his lack of female companionship and desperately wants a girlfriend. Seeing his friends and cousins marry, and then have children, has left a huge void in his life. These are things I cannot provide for John and it is excruciatingly difficult to realize I can not fulfill his needs.

It must be so difficult for John to function effectively when he is so easily over stimulated. His autism affects every aspect of his life. John chooses to overcome the many obstacles put before him each day so that he may be a contributing member of society. It would be so much easier for him to stay in the comfort of his room, where everything is predictable and ordered. When John comes home at the end of his day, he immediately heads to the safe sanctuary of his bedroom. There he is surrounded by all the things he loves and he no longer has to conform to societal standards. John is then free to be who he is, without fear of rejection.

For years, John was in denial of his disability. He didn't want to be associated with anyone he considered disabled. Heck, he didn't want to be seen with his father and mother once he was grown up and have our presence seen as inadequacy on his part. However, recently we have seen an incredible change in John. He seems to have finally accepted who he is. We speak of autism on a daily basis and I often remind John of the strengths he possesses. He has a brilliant mind, a memory I'd give my eye teeth for, and numerous talents artistically.

We watch programs on television about autism and have frequent conversations about how many people live with it each day. John's eight year old cousin has been diagnosed with autism and we are able to talk about how John felt as a child, dealing with what was then a relatively unknown disorder. With perseverance and time, John appears to be coming into his own. He has recently joined two different social groups. One group is a self-advocacy group that consists of people from diverse backgrounds who are disabled. They meet twice a month with a facilitator helping them to better understand their needs. The other group is an Asperger's support group which is comprised of about a dozen young men with high-functioning autism. They meet monthly and a facilitator encourages social interaction through games, activities and discussions. Both of these groups probably play a big part in John's new found sense of self. John enjoys the meetings, and feels comfort in acquiring new friends. I can only hope for an overflow into his life outside of the organized group. We are encouraged by the social gains John has recently made. John is fortunate to have a day program for twenty six hours a week. With a job coach's support, he is able to work, and takes an art class each Monday, goes to the gym twice a week, and enjoys many other activities in our community. We feel fortunate that we have arrived at this point of John's life relatively intact. Although there have been struggles, we have overcome them and keep an upbeat attitude. It would be easy to be lost in a sea of self-pity but we prefer to laugh rather than cry. And most of all, there is hope for light at the end of the tunnel as our journey continues.

John shares his artistic talent at his first art show, coordinated with the help of his art teacher, Darlene.

Autism

You know I'm different and you think I'm strange

There are a lot of things I cannot rearrange

Well, you may see me in the hall

Or you may see me on the street

You might pass me by each day

Even though we never meet

And I'd truly like to say

I would love to be like you

Oh so open, oh so true.

Just like that missing puzzle piece

That could make it all come through

I'm just a person trapped inside

And it's true I'd like to say

Could you please accept me anyway

Even though I'm not like you.

— A. H. Walker

Epilogue

Writing this book is, by far, the most challenging project I have ever attempted. I could never have envisioned how incredibly emotional this experience would be. As I wrote each chapter, I was reliving that period of time in our lives. There are wonderful memories, as well as times of despair included in these pages. Our family has indeed been on a journey through the Autism maze over the past almost three decades. The quote "one day at a time" is our mantra . . . it would have been impossible to make it through such an exhausting phenomenon with eyes wide open. It is absolutely necessary to just live each moment, in whatever way one is able to cope, to prevent becoming overwhelmed. It is amazing to look back and realize that our family has gone through so much and we're still alive and kicking. Even more incredible is the fact that we have not lost our minds completely in the process! I believe communication is the key to having the most successful outcome when dealing with the obstacles thrown at families living with Autism each day. There really is no going it alone, many people are constantly thrust into our lives, by way of our child's disorder. To truly reap the optimum benefits from these folks, we must keep the lines of communication open at all times.

It is with utmost importance we never lose sight of the person who has sent us on this journey. My son has taught me more than I could ever have learned in any classroom, or from any book. The experiences we have weathered together are invaluable. It's easy to get caught up in all of the strategies necessary to cope and almost forget why you are doing the things you are. The person living with Autism is the true hero . . . they are the ones who struggle each day to fit into a world they are ill-equipped for. I've always explained to John that "it's the way you're wired" which makes things so difficult. It doesn't make him any less of a person, just a very unique individual who has every right to enjoy his place in society. We have a very important mission; we must continue to educate those around us about this fascinating disorder. It is imperative people understand why our children behave the way they do and accept them for the wonderful human beings they are. We need to showcase their talents that far overshadow their weaknesses.

I am constantly being told that John would not have come as far in his life without my tireless support. While this may be somewhat true, I feel he has always been the engine pulling the train. There are many, many people who share in his success. But not any one of us could have done this alone. It is truly a group effort. The metaphor "it takes a village to raise a child" could have been conceived to explain the best way to support those with Autism. It indeed is true that everyone who comes into contact with this population can make a difference in their lives, whether they are able to make that difference a positive one is the challenge.

In today's world, Autism is so much better known than twenty-something years ago, when we first began our journey. It is my sincere hope that children today will grow up in a more accepting society where they are seen as an integral members and do not feel like they are on the outside, looking in. Let's pledge to make this happen for each child who happens to be in the one out of eighty-eight children born each day with Autism.

Dad, Mom, and John at John's best friend's wedding reception.

Acknowledgement

S her Kamman was John's psychotherapist for 22 years and without her caring support who knows where John would be now. She became my friend, as well as John's therapist. Her encouragement was paramount when I would hit a wall while writing the book, reliving some of the most difficult moments in our lives. Sher was almost as excited as we were to see this book published!

About the Author

Ellen Walker has worked as a special education paraeducator for 25 years and will be retiring in June of 2013. Along with spending more time with her family, her hope is to have time for supporting other families of children with special needs in any capacity she can. She feels that family support is a necessity, as she has witnessed during her journey with John. Ellen and Al have been married for forty years, which is an accomplishment, based on the fact that many marriages cannot survive the stress of raising a child with autism.

CPSIA information can be obtained at www.ICGtesting.com
Printed in the USA
BVOW011338100313

315091BV00008B/36/P

9 780988 537019